Marc Rolston
June 1981

PIERCE-ARROW

PIERCE-ARROW
MARC RALSTON

SAN DIEGO • NEW YORK   A.S. BARNES & COMPANY, INC.
IN LONDON: THE TANTIVY PRESS

Pierce Arrow text copyright ©1980 by A. S. Barnes and Co., Inc.
San Diego, California 92121

The Tantivy Press
Magdalen House
136-148 Tooley Street
London, SE1 2TT, England

First Edition
Manufactured in the United States of America
For information write to A. S. Barnes and Company, Inc.,
P.O. Box 3051, San Diego, CA 92038

Library of Congress Cataloging in Publication Data
Ralston, Marc, 1930–
　　Pierce Arrow.

　　Includes index.
　　1. Pierce-Arrow Automobile. 2. The Pierce-Arrow
Motor Car Company. I. Title.
TL215.P6R34　629.2'222　80-15214
ISBN 0-498-02451-2

1 2 3 4 5 6 7 8 9　84 83 82 81 80

CONTENTS

PREFACE

I suspect that my interest in old cars was kindled when I was a teenager. My father and I used to go downtown each September to view the new cars. We compared the features and styles in order to decide which car to buy, but my father was Scottish; we never bought, just looked. I have good memories of those hours shared with my father and automobiles. During many years of schooling that followed, I did not have the time, money or opportunity for my interest in cars to surface.

It probably was my daughter who was responsible for re-awakening my interest in the old cars. On a family vacation in 1972 we visited an amusement park that offered rides in reproduction Model Ts. After many rides my daughter asked, "Daddy, why don't we get an old car?" This remark, coupled with a tour through an antique auto museum, unleashed an uncontrollable and obsessive interest in antique automobiles (most doctors appear to be obsessive-compulsive personalities anyway). My wife says that in the spring my feet turn into wheels.

As with most people bitten by the antique auto "bug," my appetite for information about *all* old cars was voracious from the start. With time, a collector's interests will usually gravitate to a few marques that fulfill his particular needs. After collecting a few autos and acquiring a modicum of knowledge about them, only to find that they did not please me, I became intrigued with one of America's most prestigious automobiles—the Pierce-Arrow. Part of its appeal came from its being a high-quality, low-production automobile, with limited availability. (Pierce-Arrow hobbyists are not particularly numerous, unlike the ubiquitous Ford collectors.)

I was surprised and frustrated by the lack of a good, complete and succinct source of information on the Pierce-Arrow. The Pierce-Arrow Society is a dedicated group of Pierce-Arrow aficionados who willingly exchange information and assistance. Their publication, *The Arrow*, provides a wealth of information through its editor, Bernie Weis. Nevertheless, I sensed the need for a single publication, which would contain as much information as possible on this important marque, as has been written about so many other great American cars.

No full-length book currently is available on the Pierce-Arrow. I hope this text will serve as a useful source of information for the hobbyists.

ACKNOWLEDGMENTS

This publication has been made possible by the generous help of many people dedicated to the preservation of the great name of Pierce-Arrow. I'm very appreciative of the considerable help from Bernie Weis, editor of *The Arrow.*

The Motor Vehicle Manufacturers Association of the United States, Inc. (M.V.M.A.), has been an invaluable source of pictures, data and help. I am particularly indebted to Mr. James Wren, manager of the Patent Library of M.V.M.A., and Ms. Bernice Huffman and Ms. Shirley McMurray of the Communications Division of M.V.M.A. for their generous help.

The University of Michigan's Engineering-Transportation Library has an extensive collection of early Pierce factory photographs and original advertising watercolors. I appreciate the liberal assistance given to me by Mrs. Sharon Balius and Miss Anji Brenner at this library.

Great care has been taken to insure accuracy. But, as with any technical and historical work, errors are bound to creep in. The author would appreciate being informed of any misinformation, to set the record straight.

It is earnestly hoped that this book will help preserve the memory of that nostalgic name, which for nearly four decades was synonymous with quality, wealth, and gracious living—the Pierce-Arrow.

INTRODUCTION

With the dawn of the Industrial Revolution in the early 19th century, scientific inventions proliferated in all fields, but none was more vital to life in early America than the devices of transportation. They were the key to expanding our large country.

Robert Fulton's development of the steamboat in 1807 expedited water travel. Trains made distant travel more practical after about 1840, but horseback was still the prevalent means of local transportation. The imaginative were restlessly seeking a faster and more dependable means of travel. Cugnot of France designed a steam wagon in 1770, and an early model of this machine actually survives today in a Paris museum. In this country, Oliver Evans of Delaware was working in the 1780s on a self-propelled steam vehicle, which never came to fruition. Despite many early attempts, the perfection of a self-propelled vehicle had to wait for the state of the art to catch up with the dreams of men.

The present-day bicycle began with Baron Von Drais' Hobby Horse, invented in 1817. Michaux of France put pedals on the front wheel of a Hobby Horse in 1863 and originated the Boneshaker velocipede. But it wasn't until 1866 that a patent was granted to Pierre Lallement of the United States for a bicycle with pedals attached to the front wheels. The Highwheelers, or Penny-farthings, became popular in England after 1870. They required much skill to ride and although fast, were dangerous. In the United States, the Highwheeler was called the Ordinary. Colonel Albert A. Pope founded the Pope Manufacturing Company in 1878 to make the Columbia Ordinary. He later produced the Pope-Hartford automobile.

John Starley invented the safety bicycle (one with equal-size wheels) in England in 1884. The safety bicycle was introduced to the United States in 1888 by Colonel Pope and became tremendously popular, replacing the Ordinary. The pneumatic tire, invented by the English veterinarian J.B. Dunlop in 1888, was a boon to cycling. Tubeless tires came in 1890. The demand was so great for the bicycle that by 1899 there were 312 bicycle manufacturers in this country. The United States was becoming a nation on wheels. The early improvements in American highways were really a response to complaining cyclists, rather than to automobile drivers.

While improvements were making the bicycle a practical means of travel, the gasoline engine was being developed and refined. Nicholas Otto had a workable gasoline engine in 1877. The marriage of the bicycle, the buggy, and the gasoline engine was inevitable, and in 1885 Karl Benz drove his first three-wheel gasoline vehicle. Later that year Daimler motorized a buggy. Many men were trying to fabricate a workable self-propelled vehicle, so it is impossible to say who really "invented" the first automobile, but Benz usually is given credit. Once the floodgate opened, evryone began building a car in his back shed. Those in the bicycle, buggy, or machine-shop business had obvious advantages, and many famous marques had just such humble beginnings. Ultimately the variety of makes was to run into the thousands. In many cases there was just one model of a particular marque produced and no representative vehicle survived. The first American car is credited to the Duryea Brothers (1893), followed by Haynes-Apperson of Kokomo (July 4, 1894), while Ford and Olds each made his first car in 1896.

Along with gasoline engines, steam and electric motors were competing for acceptance as the best source of power. Hiram D. Maxim built his first Columbia electric car in 1895. The Stanley Brothers built their steam car in 1896. Slowly, the impracticality of steam and electric motors allowed the gasoline engine to win out. By World War I, steam and electric cars were uttering their terminal gasps.

The French are given credit for coining the word *automobile;* the first French auto was exported to the United States in 1897. In Europe, automobile manufacturing was further along than in the United States, and regular automobile events were held even before the turn of the century. Once the automobile appeared on the American scene, a rapid proliferation of cars occurred. There were more than 2,000 au-

tomobiles in the United States before 1900. U.S. production in 1900 was more than 4,000 vehicles, and by 1910 the annual production exceeded 180,000. America's first automobile show of new cars was held November 3, 1900, in New York City's Madison Square Garden with forty makers exhibiting. Of these, only Rambler (AMC) survives today.

These were exciting times of rapid industrial change, when the George N. Pierce Company had its beginning. It grew with the young industry, rising to the top with an uncompromising dedication to producing the finest automobile possible. By World War I the Pierce-Arrow was undoubtedly the most prestigious American car. Its mere name evoked images of Edwardian splendor and all of the sophistication that wealth could buy. Then, like the dinosaur, unable to adapt to change, it slowly died. The company, reflecting the character of its founders, would never compromise quality nor make a "cheap" car, and that was its final undoing during the Depression. During its years of leadership it was the forerunner in aluminum bodies, dual-valve engines, power brakes, and hydraulic tappets. Now, almost forty years after the company went into bankruptcy, fewer than 2,000 vehicles survive among the approximately 85,000 manufactured. The heirs to that great tradition are the collectors who preserve and restore those grand cars, which recall a time of opulence and gracious living.

PIERCE-ARROW

VICTORY FOLLOWS VICTORY

=>PIERCE=>

Pierce Single Cylinder and Four Cylinder Models have won victories **in ever** **endurance contest ever entered.** The more recent triumphs are:

Cleveland Endurance Run, May 28th, 29th, 30th—2 Perfect Scores
Philadelphia to Atlantic City, June 26th . . . . . —2 Perfect Scores
San Francisco Endurance Run, July 2d, 3d . . . . —1 Perfect Score
Scranton Hill Climb, July 1st . . . . —1 Perfect Score
GRAND PRIZE.—Buenos Aires Centennial Exposition, 1911 (International
    Competition—Pierce receives sole award).

Besides the above recorded records, Pierce machines have otherwise won fame for themselves, particularly in everyday service and we are justified in claiming to have the very finest product on the world's market.

Dealers and riders should write us today. We can convince you of Pierce superiority and the advantages of doing business with us.

We also offer for sale Pierce bicycles which have won
eighty-five per cent. of all speed records in the world

EVERYONE SHOULD HAVE OUR CATALOGUE "G"

THE PIERCE CYCLE CO., BUFFALO, N. Y

PACIFIC COAST BRANCH, OAKLAND, CAL.

1
THE
BEGINNING
1846–78

The year was 1846. James Polk was President. The United States was at war with Mexico. The Smithsonian Institution had just been founded. The first anesthetic was being used in medicine by Doctor Morton, and George Norman Pierce was born (January 9) in Friendsville, Pennsylvania, a small farming community just south of Endicott, New York.

George's father, Henry Pierce, was a merchant and farmer, and his maternal ancestors dated back to the *Mayflower* colonists. His grandfather, John Harvey Pierce, of Axminster, England, had been physician to the Crown. As a youth, George did not want for a good education, attending public school, the Waverly Academy across the state line, thirty miles from home, and the Bryant and Stratton Business College in Buffalo. In 1863, at seventeen, he landed his first job at the Townsend Manufacturing Company in Buffalo. Later he moved to the John C. Javett Manufacturing Company. George was an aggressive and honest businessman. These qualities, in the expanding frontiers of science, brought him success (marrying well did not hurt him either). He did not, however, gain great wealth through his company. Money became available through his marriage on October 21, 1875, to Louisa Day. She was the daughter of Moses Day, a manufacturer of rope from Roxbury, Massachusetts. Moses Day had invented a process for making rope of continuous length, and she had inherited

considerable money from her father.

Eager to move ahead on his own, George left the Javett Company, and at twenty-seven helped establish the firm of Heintz, Pierce, and Munschauer. Here he gained manufacturing experience while making birdcages, ice boxes, tin ware, washing machines, and other small household items (the first ammonia refrigerators were built in 1873 in Germany). After only three years in the partnership, he left that firm in 1876. He had been the son-in-law of Moses Day less than a year. Two years later, at thirty-two, he formed his own business, the George N. Pierce Company in 1878. His company continued to make birdcages, refrigerators, and ice chests, and in 1888 also began producing children's tricycles. The year 1878 also saw the development of the Edison phonograph, followed the next year by the electric light. With his own business, Pierce now had the facilities for branching out into other areas.

Bicycles (1892–1914)

The George N. Pierce Company was a financial success. As early as 1889 an advertisement in *The Iron Age* shows the company selling the Queen tricycle in twenty varieties. Ladies, unable to ride the large Ordinary bicycle, rode the smaller tricycles. The firm's different styles of ice chests numbered 167. Even in this early period Pierce demonstrated his zeal for making too many models. Twenty-five years later this practice jeopardized the company. By 1892 Pierce was building bicycles exclusively; by then they had become the rage in the United States. The manufacturing of birdcages and refrigerators was discontinued in 1895. Surviving bicycles are stamped with patent dates from 1886 through 1898, which suggests that Pierce may have been building the bicycle even before 1892. Through national advertising, the firm became one of the leaders in bicycle manufacturing, known both for quality and large scale production. The established bicycle dealer outlets were to be very useful later in promoting the Pierce automobile.

The name of Frank L. Kramer, American Champion bicyclist, was used to promote sales in magazine ads after the turn of the century. The Pierce escutcheon, with the superimposed arrow, first adorned the bicycles and was later modified to become the company's famous logo. The bicycles were available with such superior equipment as the sprung-rear frame, and either chain or shaft drive with bevel gear. The precision-ground gears came from the Leland and Faulconer foundry in Detroit, a firm with a reputation in the United States for quality castings. Henry Leland later was to be on the Board of Directors of the new Cadillac Automobile Company, and he helped design the early one-cylinder Cadillac. Later this firm would supply high-cost and superior-quality engine cylinders for the Pierce-Arrow Company engines. George Pierce's dedication to the best materials and workmanship soon earned his bicycle a reputation of quality. This creed continued throughout the years of manufacturing automobiles. An 1899 bicycle brochure listed models priced from $50 to $85, with Morrow coaster brakes available for $10 extra.

The production of bicycles was separated from automobile manufacturing with the formation of the Pierce Cycle Company in September, 1907. Percy P. Pierce, son of George Pierce, became president. George Pierce had nine children, but only Percy was noted for his interest in the family business. Besides building bicycles, young Pierce introduced a four-cylinder motorcycle in 1909, reportedly after two years of development work. The quality of the motorcycle was commensurate with the Pierce reputation, and the price was an equally-impressive $325. Although the cycle was well received, the price was considerably higher than that of the competition, and

pressure was brought to bear to issue a less expensive machine.

In 1910 the answer was a large one-cylinder motorcycle that sold for $250, still no small sum. The bore and stroke were 2³/₁₆″ x 2¹/₂″ for the four-cylinder and 3¹/₂″ x 4″ for the single-cylinder model. The advertising touted the four-cylinder engine as the "vibrationless motorcycle," and it was a well-designed machine.

In 1910 a two-speed gearbox and clutch were introduced on the "4." In 1911 and 1912 other models were available, with better features and higher prices. The price tag of $400 hurt sales. And although Pierce motorcycles were winning many endurance runs, profits sagged.

By 1913 the costly-to-produce Pierce motorcycle brought financial problems to the Pierce Cycle Company. Perhaps a few cycles were produced in early 1914, but in effect 1913 was the last year of a production model.

There were efforts to refinance the company, but foreclosure by the banks eventually brought bankruptcy. Ironically, the company had orders at that time from the Japanese government for 7,000 bicycles, but could not obtain the money from the bank to fill them. Sadly, all production came to a halt. After bankruptcy, the Pierce Cycle Company was bought out by the Emblem Manufacturing Company of Angola, New York, which continued to manufacture bicycles into the 1930s. The same Pierce escutcheon was used, but the new company name was imprinted on it.

During the five-year period that the motorcycles were built, it is estimated that about 8,500 were turned out. The Pierce-Arrow Society Roster lists less than fifteen survivors. In twenty years of manufacturing bicycles, approximately three dozen are presently accounted for. These rare machines are eagerly sought by collectors.

Growth of the Company

In 1896, after four good years in the bicycle business, the George N. Pierce Company became incorporated with George Pierce, now fifty, as president. Henry May was vice president in charge of manufacturing, and Colonel Charles Clifton was treasurer. The secretary was Lawrence H. Gardner, who first joined the Pierce Company in 1886 along with William H. Gardner, a member of the board of directors.

George K. Birge, a graduate of Cornell, was also an officer on the board of directors. His father had founded the M.H. Birge and Sons Company, which was a large wallpaper firm in Buffalo (that company is still making wallpaper). After succeeding his father in that business, he had become wealthy and had put a lot of money into the George N. Pierce Company. Birge was socially prominent in the Buffalo area and was a patron of the arts. The man was short, soft-spoken, and well-dressed. As George Pierce's health began to fail, Birge became quite active in managing the Pierce Company. Later, after George Pierce's retirement in 1909, Birge was to become president of the company, a post that he held from 1910 until 1916.

William B. Hoyt was the company's legal advisor and also sat on the board of directors. He was intelligent and tough, but a gracious gentleman. He had been an attorney for the Vanderbilt Railroad.

Henry May first joined the firm of Heintz, Pierce, and Munschauer at twelve, in 1873, as an errand boy. He attended night school and worked hard to rise through the company ranks to become sales manager. By 1887, he was a partner in the George N. Pierce Company. With its incorporation in 1896, he became vice president in charge of manufacturing. He was remembered as a large man, who was all business but well-respected for his ability. He was the one who made the factory "go" and was a power behind the success of the Pierce Company.

Colonel Charles Clifton (1853–1928) was the "grand old man" of Pierce-Arrow. Charming and intelligent, he was a strong force in guiding the direction and philosophy of the company during his thirty years there. Born in Buffalo, he was a self-made man, starting as a clerk in a hardware store in Buffalo, then working as a coal dealer. At a young age, he became treasurer of the George N. Pierce Company, later to become president for a brief period (1916–18). He, too, was a prominent business figure and a patron of the arts. He was associated with the University of Buffalo and the Buffalo Fine Arts Academy. His influence on the management and philosophy of the company, and the entire automobile industry, was considerable, and he was president of the National Automobile Manufacturers Association from 1912 to 1927.

These were the men who formed the company in 1896 and guided its philosophy in the early years. They were gentlemen of integrity, wealth, and culture, and the quality of their product reflected their character.

The George N. Pierce Company's first home was a five-story factory with 75,000 square feet located at 18 Hanover Street in Buffalo, New York. The date when they first occupied that location is obscure.

Before 1900, there had been very few American cars built (Duryea 1893, Haynes-Apperson 1894, Ford 1896, Olds 1897, Locomobile 1899, and Packard 1899). In 1896 Duryea sold to George Morill of Massachusetts the first of his thirteen "production" cars. While George Pierce and Henry May were working hard in the bicycle business, Colonel Clifton began looking toward that new toy, the automobile. Before 1900 the board of directors decided that the company should look into the new field of automobiles, and the building of an experimental car was authorized. An article in a Buffalo newspaper, circa 1908, stated that Pierce began experimenting with automobiles as early as 1898. A Pierce publication, dated 1904, states that Pierce built six Overman steam cars during 1900. It also says that experimentation on a gasoline engine was carried out between 1898 and 1900. The Pierce Racine automobile, built between 1903 and 1911 in Racine, Wisconsin, was produced by Andrew James Pierce and was not related to the Pierce-Arrow. The Pierce Racine became the Case automobile after 1911.

In 1900, Percy Pierce, F.A. Nickerson and Ephraim Bowen began building trial steam cars. The first trial run on August 21, 1900, ended with a broken axle. More trials, generally unsuccessful, were made in the following months, and Pierce, Nickerson and Bowen soon abandoned their steam automobile as impractical.

In the meantime, Colonel Clifton had travelled to Europe to investigate the refinements in European automobiles. It was conceded that the French automobiles were more advanced than the American machines. The name of Panhard et Levassor was already well-known and respected. Clifton returned, favoring the use of the deDion one-cylinder gasoline engine, and that engine was used in further experiments on a gasoline-powered vehicle in the winter of 1900. The first trial run on the prototype was made on November 24, 1900. The design was a four-wheel, two-seat, buggy-style vehicle with a one-cylinder deDion engine and cone friction clutch. Riding along with Percy Pierce in that first trial run was Charles Sheppy, who was destined to be chief engineer at Pierce-Arrow from 1921–1927. It is not known what happened to this first experimental vehicle.

The Motorette (1901–3)

During this time, while the first Pierce car was being built, David Fergusson, who was to become instrumental in the development of the early Pierce automobiles as the first chief engineer, arrived on the scene. Fergusson was born in 1869 (and died in 1951) in Yorkshire, England. He was graduated from Bradford Technical College in 1889. For eight years he gathered mechanical experience while working in gasoline engine and steam locomotive shops. Immigrating to the United States, he moved to Syracuse, New York, to work for the E.C. Stearns Company, which was experimenting with steam vehicles. Being a strong proponent of gasoline engines over steam, but unable to sway the company to his experimental gasoline model, he left Syracuse and went to Pierce to try to convince the board of directors of the superiority of gasoline-powered automobiles. As a result of his efforts, he was hired to design and build two gasoline automobiles for the Pierce Company, beginning on February 4, 1901. He remained the chief engineer of the Pierce Company until he left in 1921 to go to Cunningham, in Rochester.

David Fergusson's first two prototype cars were patterned after the French two-passenger Motorette and were driven by deDion $2^5/16''$ x $3''$ one-cylinder vertical engines that had been imported from France by Colonel Clifton. The cars had two forward speeds but no reverse. The buggy-type body had 26-inch wire wheels and weighed 600 pounds. By May 1, 1901, after three months work, the first two cars were completed and ready for trial. In the following months, these cars were driven about and tested. By fall of 1901 they were ready to be entered in the endurance run from New York City to Buffalo, October 7 to 15. In their first contest, both of the cars (Numbers A-7 and A-8) held up well and finished the race, winning second class certificates. Their average speed was 10½ miles per hour! Pictures of these two Motorettes were featured in a 1901 Pierce brochure that described their first Model A. Pierce-made cars were to win many endurance races. The early races were valuable to the manufacturers, not only as a means of evaluating and refining their machines, but also as a very profitable way to publicize their automobiles. Consequently, much time, effort and money were directed towards such contests as the Glidden Tour, the 1908 New York to Paris race won by Thomas Flyer, the Dewar Trophy, and the Vanderbilt cup.

During that first production year of 1901–02 only twenty-five autos, similar to the two experimental cars, were built. They were priced at $650. A surviving model was repurchased in 1916 by the Pierce-Arrow Company and displayed at its Elmwood Showroom. In 1926 it was donated to the Buffalo Historical Society. Later it was restored by Pierce-Arrow Society member Peter Lapey.

George N. Pierce (1846–1910). (Courtesy of the Pierce-Arrow Society.)

Top—Pierce advertisement from *Iron Age*, March 1888. (Courtesy of Jim Gebhardt.) *Center*—Pierce advertisement from *The Metal Worker*, June 1890. (Courtesy of Jim Gebhardt.) *Bottom*—Pierce bicycle advertisement from *The Century Illustrated Monthly Magazine*, July 1901. (Courtesy of the Pierce-Arrow Society.)

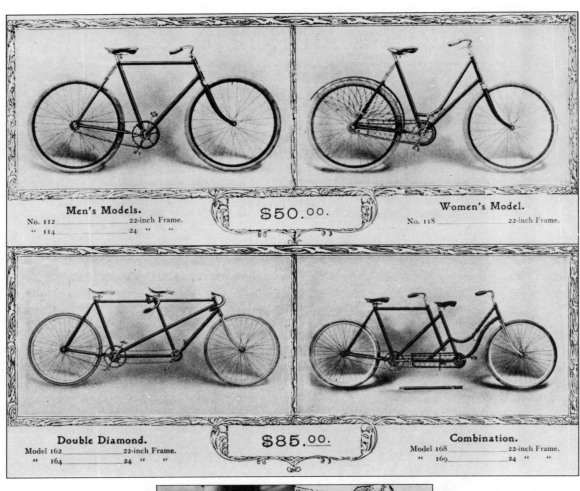

Men's Models.

No. 112   22-inch Frame.
"   114   24 " "

$50.00.

Women's Model.

No. 118   22-inch Frame.

Double Diamond.

Model 162   22-inch Frame.
"   164   24 " "

$85.00.

Combination.

Model 168   22-inch Frame.
"   169   24 " "

Top and center — Different Pierce bicycle models from an 1899 catalog. (Courtesy of the University of Michigan.)
Bottom left — The Pierce bicycle emblem (circa 1900) utilizing the arrow. *Bottom right* — Frank Kramer
raced and promoted Pierce bicycles as shown in this 1902 advertisement in *The American Boy*.
(Courtesy of the Pierce-Arrow Society.)

Top—The Pierce four-cylinder motorcycle first produced in 1909. (Courtesy of the Pierce-Arrow Society.)
Bottom—The less expensive one-cylinder model introduced in 1910. (Courtesy of the Pierce-Arrow Society.)

Top left—Henry May, vice president of Pierce-Arrow from 1896 until 1916. (Courtesy of the Pierce-Arrow Society.) *Top right*—George K. Birge (1849–1918), president of the Pierce-Arrow Motor Car Company from 1910 to 1916. (Courtesy of Bernie Weis.) *Center left*—Lawrence H. Gardner, first secretary of the George N. Pierce Company. (Courtesy of Bernie Weis.) *Center middle*— David Fergusson (1869–1950), the first chief engineer of the George N. Pierce Company. (Courtesy of Bernie Weis.) *Center right*—Colonel Charles Clifton (1853–1928), treasurer of the George N. Pierce Company from 1896 to 1916, and president from 1916 to 1918. (Courtesy of the Pierce-Arrow Society.) *Bottom*—The first George N. Pierce Company factory at 18 Hanover Street, Buffalo, New York (photo circa 1901). After 1906 this building was the site of bicycle fabrication. (Courtesy of the Pierce-Arrow Society.)

During that first production year of 1901–02 only twenty-five autos, similar to the two experimental cars, were built. They were priced at $650. A surviving model was repurchased in 1916 by the Pierce-Arrow Company and displayed at its Elmwood Showroom. In 1926 it was donated to the Buffalo Historical Society

Top—The first Pierce Motorette before delivery in 1930 to the Buffalo Historical Society, where it is presently on display. Driver Edward C. Bull sold Pierce bicycles and sold the first Motorette in Buffalo. (Courtesy of the Pierce-Arrow Society.) *Bottom*—The first Pierce Motorette (1901) on display at the Buffalo Historical Society. The ribbed armrests are characteristic of the first model. (Courtesy of the Pierce-Arrow Society.)

The Pierce Arrow

NO feature of the Pierce-Arrow car has been exploited at the expense of any other feature. Well-balanced design is characteristic of both its construction and its appearance.

THE PIERCE-ARROW MOTOR CAR COMPANY, BUFFALO, N. Y.
Members Association Licensed Automobile Manufacturers.

2
THE
GREAT RACE
1900–04

It was as if the turn of the century were the starting gun; the great automobile race was off and running. At first the new industry's growth was slow and faltering. Although Henry Ford had built his first car in June 1896, he was to fail in his first three attempts to make a commercial production automobile. It wasn't until 1903 that the very successful Ford Motor Company was formed. Ransom E. Olds also made his first auto in 1896. By 1899 the Olds Motor Works was producing gasoline automobiles. In 1901 the factory was swept by fire, and only a prototype Olds was saved; when the plant resumed production, this "curved-dash" Olds was the only model manufactured. It was immediately accepted by the public as a very popular auto. Within four years more than 6,000 were being built annually. After much financial difficulty, David Buick, the developer of the porcelainized bathtub, was able to form his own company to begin building experimental cars in 1903. The company was successful and became the hub of General Motors, but its originator was destined to spend the rest of his life in a series of failures outside of the company, which he left in 1906. The Locomobile Company was formed in June 1899, and the first Packard was born November 6, 1899.

Not to be outdone by the young, struggling companies, the government got into the act. In 1901 New York started requiring annual registration of automobiles for one dollar, and the other states soon followed suit. At first, license plates consisted of the owner's initials placed on leather or metal plates of the owner's choosing. In 1903 Massachusetts became the first state to issue license plates. Then other states began issuing their own plates, first on porcelainized metal and then from stamped steel. Collecting old license plates has become a popular hobby in its own right.

To aid the new fraternity of motorists, automobile clubs sprang up throughout the country. By 1901 there were thirty-six auto clubs in the United States. That same year thirty of the clubs joined to form the American Automobile Association (AAA).

It was estimated that, at the turn of the century, less than 200 miles of paved rural road existed; most roads were dirt or mud. Motoring was for those with pioneering spirit, not for the faint-hearted. The first transcontinental automobile trip in July 1903 must have been quite an adventure.

The first president of the United States to ride in an automobile (a Stanley Steamer) was McKinley. Five years after McKinley was assassinated while visiting the 1901 Pan-American Exposition in Buffalo, New York, the sixteen-acre area that had been the site of the Exposition was purchased by the expanding George

N. Pierce Company for its new Elmwood plant.

It was during these rapidly changing times in the automobile world that the Pierce Company had its beginning.

The First Pierce Automobiles (1901–3)
First (A–D), Second (D, E, F), and Third (F, G, H, K) Models

Automobiles were not very useful at first; they were regarded as playthings of the wealthy, and not as a serious means of travel. At the beginning of the century a new industry was developing from a rich man's toy. George Pierce had built two experimental gasoline-driven Motorettes by May 1901, and trials showed them to be very reliable automobiles. These Motorettes (first model, or Model A) were built until May 1902. They were hardly more than buggies driven by a one-cylinder $2\frac{3}{4}$-horsepower deDion engine imported from France. The small engine was mounted vertically beneath the driver's seat. The bore and stroke were $2^{15}/_{16}''$ x $3''$. The starting crank on the right side was connected with the engine by means of a bicycle chain. The Motorette carried two people and had two forward gears but no reverse. Steering was done by means of a horizontal tiller that could be swung to the right or left side. The speed-governing lever and spark advance were mounted on the tiller column. The car had a spur-gear drive, 26-inch wheels, a weight of 600 pounds, and a top speed of about 20 miles per hour; at 30 miles per gallon it could travel about 80 miles. Of the twenty-five units made before May 1902, only the first car survived and is on display in the Buffalo Historical Society museum.

The cover of a 1901 Pierce sales pamphlet shows car A-7 (presumably the seventh car hand-fabricated,) with an unknown man riding in Delaware Park in Buffalo. Also pictured in the pamphlet are the two 1901 New York to Buffalo Endurance Contest entrants, cars A-7 and A-8. Pierce received a second class award in that contest and was greatly encouraged by the success of the company's first venture into the automotive field.

The 1901 pamphlet lists two models. The first (car A-7) is the Knockabout described above, which can be recognized by the beveled edges on the front of the body. The 1919 Pierce Recension Table refers to this model as 2.75D. The second (car A-8) was the Runabout model, weighing about 750 pounds and driven

by a slightly larger $3\frac{1}{2}$-horsepower one-cylinder deDion engine. This Runabout probably corresponds to the second model, or 3.5 D-E model as described in the 1919 Pierce Recension Table, and could be considered nominally a 1902 car. This model had two forward speeds and a reverse gear. The water-cooled engine had a $3^{5}/_{32}''$ x $3^{5}/_{32}''$ bore and stroke. The body was similar to that of the smaller Knockabout, with the addition of two front headlights and a top available at extra cost. This Motorette had a top speed of 25 miles per hour, which was rather impressive for 1902. About 125 Motorettes of this Runabout model were built all during 1902 and into early 1903. They were well-made and reliable, and sold well. The price was $850 for the larger Runabout. A 1902 Pierce brochure shows a patent number 549,160 dated November 5, 1895. An old newspaper article suggests that Pierce might have been experimenting with automobiles before the generally accepted date of 1900.

If deDion could make a good gasoline engine, then George Pierce could make a better one. Development was begun in 1902, and by early 1903 the deDion engine was replaced by a 5-horsepower one-cylinder Pierce-built engine (Pierce Patent 704699, July 15, 1902). Bore and stroke were $3^{3}/_{8}''$ x $3^{9}/_{16}''$. Pierce data referred to this as their third model or 5 H-K. The one-cylinder engine, cast by Leland and Faulconer Foundry of Detroit, was of good quality and expensive. The body was larger and roomier but still held only two passengers. The diameter of the wire wheels was increased to 28 inches, and a third headlight was added in the center. Otherwise, the car was mechanically similar to the two previous models. The weight was about 800 pounds; the price was $950. About forty were made before that model was discontinued later in 1903. The total production of the Motorette between 1901 and 1903 was approximately 170 automobiles; of these, six are listed in the Pierce-Arrow Society Roster at this writing. With this model the George N. Pierce Company established itself as a builder of a reliable production automobile. The already-established bicycle dealers aided in the distribution of the auto and helped make it a commercial success. However, the characteristics of this vehicle limited its usefulness and soon made it obsolete. In response to public demand, Pierce began work on a series of new and improved models.

The Stanhope Motorette (1903–6)
Fourth (6-6½-H-K), Fifth (8-L), and Seventh (8-M) Models

Experimentation and endurance tests brought out the shortcomings in the Motorette. The Stanhope fourth model, or 6-6½-H-K, was introduced later in 1903 to carry more passengers. Its buggy-type body was similar to that of the Motorette, except that a fold-out seat was added in front of the driver's seat so that two additional passengers could be carried. Fergusson said that the additional seat was intended for emergency use. The engine beneath the driver's seat was enlarged to a 6½-horsepower single-cylinder, vertical Pierce-made engine with bore increased to 3⁹/₁₆ inches and stroke to 4⁵/₁₆ inches. Other features were similar to the Motorette's, with two forward speeds and reverse, a steering lever, and a folding Victoria top. The 28-inch wheels were changed to the wooden spoked type. The car cost $1,200; the top, with round side window, was available for $100 extra. Weight was 1,200 pounds. One hundred forty-nine were made during 1903.

In late 1903, the horsepower was increased to 8 in Stanhope fifth model, or 8-L. There it stayed until better designs forced the Stanhope to be phased out three years later. The size of the wooden wheels was increased to 30 inches with a 3-inch tire; the car's weight was 1,250 pounds. The Stanhope was available only in Quaker green with black and gold trimmings. The wheelbase was 70 inches, and the tread was 54 inches with a tubular frame. A planetary transmission was used, with two forward gears and a reverse gear. The gasoline tank held only 5½ gallons, but the one-cylinder engine would take the car about 150 miles. The price with top was $1,275, and fifty-one were produced.

The 1904 seventh model, or 8-M, was similar to the previous year's Model 8-L (still with the 8-horsepower engine), except that the tiller steering was replaced by a steering wheel, and the Victoria top now had a rectangular window instead of a round one. This transition to a steering wheel occurred in late 1903. Surviving car number 321, nominally a 1903, has a steering wheel. A canopy top with front glass window and leather side curtains was also available. Four different leather tops were available for an extra $85 to $150. The model 8-M was available through 1905 and was discontinued in 1906. Because there

was more demand for larger cars, some of the later Stanhopes were dismantled, so it is difficult to be sure exactly how many were actually made in 1904 and 1905. Probably less than 220 were produced.

Although the fold-out front seat allowed for two additional passengers, their presence blocked the view of the driver. The extra weight in the front also made steering difficult. This led to the conventional French Panhard style of placing the engine in front, with the passenger seat behind the driver. Between 1903 and 1905, when the Stanhope went out of production, about 422 autos were built. At the present time seven of these are accounted for. The Pierce-Arrow Society Roster lists approximately 1,000 surviving cars totally. It is estimated that about the same number exists outside of the roster.

The Arrow (1903–6)
Sixth Model—15-J

The Stanhope model of 1903 extended the small Motorette's survival for three more years, but it was still essentially just a motorized buggy. That same year, a totally new design was developed and put into production. This was the Arrow, sixth model, or 15-J, which was a conventional automobile of the Panhard design. This was also the Pierce Company's first step in the evolution of its magnificent Great Arrow, which soon followed. The public demand was for heavier, more powerful cars; cars that could carry a large family. The Pierce Company would make them.

In late 1902 David Fergusson designed an automobile with a two-cylinder, 15-horsepower deDion engine (3¹⁵/₁₆″ x 4⁵/₁₆″) mounted in the front, with the driver and passengers behind. It carried four people, with an extra seat for a child, and had a detachable, rear-entrance tonneau body. Like the Motorette, it still had a tubular frame. The wheelbase was 81 inches. It had three forward speeds and reverse using a bevel-gear transmission. The gearshift was mounted on the steering column. The brake worked on the countershaft, while the parking brake applied to both rear wheels. The wheels were 32-inch artillery type with 3½-inch Goodrich tires. The hood with seven louvers could be raised, and had a Renault look. The weight was increased to 1,800 pounds, and the cost was a staggering $2,500. This car was exhibited in New York in January 1903. With this model the George N. Pierce Company was headed towards the prestige automobile market. Only fifty units were produced in 1903; one survives today.

Eighth Model—15-J

In 1904 the Arrow was modified to become the eighth model. It utilized a slightly larger 2-cylinder, 15-horsepower vertical *Pierce* engine with 3¹⁵/₁₆-inch bore and 4³/₄-inch stroke. The dark blue body was still a rear-entrance tonneau with an extra folding seat for a child, but the seats were now fancier tufted leather. The weight was 1,900 pounds, and it carried a 10-gallon gasoline tank. The hood was changed from the Renault look to a vertical and square Whitlock radiator. A big improvement was a fan and water pump that extended the "water range" to 400 miles. This model had fourteen louvers on the flat top and sides of the hood.

Available information published by Pierce is confusing, but apparently late in 1904 the hood of the eighth model Arrow was changed to a rounded hood with 14 louvers on top, characteristic of the 1904 Great Arrow. The hood of the 1904 Great Arrow had 16 louvers. The price of the 15-J remained $2,500. Seventy-five cars of this model were built during 1904, and one survives. The three variations of this Model 15-J were produced only during 1903 and 1904. During this period a new model was being designed, to be introduced in 1904, which would replace the relatively small Arrow model. Designs were being changed frequently. It took ten years of production for a design to become relatively stable. Between 1901 and 1907, the company went from a one-cylinder engine to a two-cylinder, then a four-cylinder, and eventually to a six-cylinder engine. The bodies increased in size correspondingly.

New York–Pittsburgh Endurance Run (1903)

In the first decade of automobile building the Pierce Company entered and won numerous contests. One early and important test was the 800-mile New York to Pittsburgh Endurance Test, which started October 7, 1903, and ran for eight days. It was a week of heavy rains and fog. This was a grueling event over washed-out roads. Only twenty of the thirty-four entrants finished the race. The details of the race were recounted by Victor Speer in the Pierce Company publication "A Tale of Triumph."

Three Pierce cars were entered. Percy Pierce and George Ulrich, who was Percy's mechanic, drove an eight-horsepower Stanhope fifth model, 8-L, winning both a second place and a gold medal. Charles Sheppy, then consulting engineer with the company, and Herman May drove a 1904 eighth model, 15-J Arrow with a two-cylinder Pierce 15-horsepower engine and came in fourth. Fred Nickerson raced in an earlier sixth model, 15-J Arrow with a two-cylinder deDion engine, to win the event for a gold medal. All three models acquitted themselves well, but a better car was yet to come.

The Great Arrow (1904)
Ninth Model—24-28N

The industry's race toward larger, faster, more powerful and better cars led the Pierce Company to bring out the ninth model Great Arrow in 1904, making a total of nine models in a four-year period. It was developed from, and looked similar to, its predecessor, the Arrow. This was a beautiful, fairly large touring car with a 93-inch wheelbase and a five-passenger rear entrance tonneau body. A 24 to 28 horsepower Pierce-built engine of four cylinders, cast in pairs, with 3¹⁵/₁₆-inch bore and 4³/₄-inch stroke was mounted in a frame of pressed steel; the weight was 2,600 pounds. The three forward and reverse speeds operated through a sliding-gear transmission with the gearshift on the steering wheel. The only color offered was Quaker green. Also new with the Great Arrow was a cast-aluminum body develope by designer James R. Way. Foundry refinements made it possible to cast the aluminum sections one-eighth-inch thick. The castings were lightweight but sturdy, and they minimized cracking in the early non-elastic paints. The sections were riveted together and finished so that the joints were imperceptible. Cast aluminum was used until 1921, when the company switched to sheet aluminum. The hood of the Great Arrow had sixteen louvers on the top and sides.

The 1904 24-28 horsepower Great Arrow won several contests, including the first AAA tour to St. Louis.

This prestigious piece of machinery cost $4,000 and the available canopy top and windshield were $250 extra. Of this Model 24-28N, only fifty cars were built, but they set the style for the next ten years at Pierce, and the basic idea was merely refined in subsequent models. One example survives.

Pierce-Arrow Awards and Records

1901 New York to Buffalo, October 7 to 15. Second-class Certificate awarded to Pierce Motorette, 2¾ horsepower.

1902 Long Island Automobile Club Endurance Run, April 26. Blue Ribbon awarded to Pierce Motorette, 3½ horsepower.

1902 Automobile Club of America Endurance Run, May 30. Blue Ribbon awarded to Pierce Motorette, 3½ horsepower.

1902 Gasoline Consumption Test, and Silver Cup, Chicago Automobile Club Endurance Run, August 2. Blue Ribbon awarded to Pierce Motorette, 3½ horsepower.

1902 Automobile Club of America, Reliability Run, New York to Boston and return, October 9 to 15. Two First-class Certificates awarded to Pierce Motorettes, 5 horsepower.

1903 New York-Pittsburgh Endurance Test, October 7 to 15. Second place on run points. Gold Medal awarded to Pierce-Stanhope, 8 horsepower.

1903 New York-Pittsburgh Endurance Test, October 7 to 15. Fourth place on run points. Gold Medal awarded to Arrow Motor Car, 15 horsepower.

1904 Mount Washington Hill-climbing Contest, July 12. Silver Medal awarded to Great Arrow, 24-28 horsepower.

1904 Mount Washington Endurance Tour, July 11 to 16. Gold Medal awarded to Great Arrow, 24-28 horsepower.

1904 First Annual Tour of the American Automobile Association, Boston to St. Louis, July 27 to August 10. First-class Certificate awarded Great Arrow Car, 24-28 horsepower.

1904 Grand Prize Louisiana Purchase Exposition.

1905 Second Annual Tour of the American Automobile Association, comprising the first contest for the Glidden Trophy, New York to White Mountains and return. Trophy won by Great Arrow Car, 28 horsepower, 1,000 miles without adjustment or repair.

1906 Third Annual Tour of the American Automobile Association, Buffalo to Bretton Woods, New Hampshire, via Saratoga, Lake Champlain, Montreal and Quebec, 1,200 miles. A Pierce Great Arrow Car defended and held the Glidden Trophy with perfect score.

1906 In the Herkomer Contest in Germany, a Great Arrow Car, 40-50 horsepower, four-cylinder, was awarded a Silver Medallion for a perfect score.

1906 Chicago Motor Club, First Annual Algonquin Hill Climb, September 6. Won, in heavy touring car class, by Pierce Great Arrow, 28-32 horsepower model.

1906 Chicago Motor Club, First Annual Economy Run, October 18. Won by Pierce Great Arrow, 28-32 horsepower model.

1907 Fourth Annual Tour of the American Automobile Association, Cleveland to New York, via Chicago, Indianapolis, Pittsburgh, Baltimore and Philadelphia, 1,570 miles. Four Great Arrow cars finished with perfect scores, two being in the team which won the Glidden Trophy for the Automobile Club of Buffalo.

1907 Chicago Motor Club's Reliability Contest, June 28. Team Prize won by Great Arrow Team, consisting of 30, 40 and 60 horsepower models.

1907 Chicago Motor Club's Second Annual Economy Run, September 13. Won by Great Arrow, 30 horsepower model.

1907 Chicago Motor Club's 200-Mile Economy Run for Knight Trophy, October 18. Won by Pierce Great Arrow, 40 horsepower, six-cylinder model.

1908 American Automobile Association Tour for the Glidden Trophy, Buffalo to Saratoga Springs, via Cleveland, Pittsburgh, Philadelphia, Albany, Boston, Poland, Maine, and Bethlehem, New Hampshire, 1,670 miles. Three Pierce-Arrow Cars (60 horsepower, six-cylinder) finished individually with perfect scores, and as a team won the Glidden Trophy.

1908 American Automobile Association Tour for the Hower Trophy for runabouts, Buffalo to Saratoga Springs (via route as above and continued to Bedford Springs, Pennsylvania, to eliminate ties, a total of 2,310 miles). Two Pierce-Arrow Runabouts (40-

horsepower, six-cylinder) finished with perfect scores, winning the Hower Trophy.

1908 Chicago Motor Club's Third Annual Alogonquin Hill Climb, August 14. Won, in heavy touring car class, by Pierce-Arrow Car, 48 horsepower, six-cylinder model.

1908 Chicago Motor Club's 1,000 Mile Reliability Contest, October 6, 7, 8 and 9. Pierce-Arrow Touring Car, 60 horsepower, six-cylinder model, finished with perfect score, winning Class "H." A Pierce-Arrow, 40 horsepower, six-cylinder runabout, in same contest was penalized one (1) point for missing fan belt, lost the first day; car was driven for three days without fan operating, finishing with otherwise perfect score.

1909 American Automobile Association Tour for the Glidden Trophy, July 12 to 30, Detroit to Kansas City, via Chicago, Minneapolis, Council Bluffs, Denver and Oakley, 2,637 miles. A 48 horsepower, 7 passenger Pierce-Arrow touring car completed the tour with a perfect road score and a perfect mechanical score, wining the Glidden Trophy.

1909 American Automobile Association Tour for the Hower Trophy, Detroit to Kansas City, 2,637 miles over route mentioned above, a 36 horsepower, 3 passenger runabout completed the tour with a perfect road score and a perfect mechanical score, winning the Hower Trophy.

Advertisements

Interestingly, with the company's evolution toward the luxury-car field starting with the Great Arrow, there also evolved a complete change in its advertising. The early ads were essentially technical in nature, showing the model and giving statistics. With the Great Arrow, about 1907 the appeal became based on the marque's association with "gentle people" of means, with minimal technical information. Often the picture included only the company name. The company rarely used actual photographs of the automobiles, relying instead on artists' renderings. This started a new trend in automobile advertising. The viewer was to associate the Pierce automobile with wealth and taste. These pictures were done in lovely watercolors by Louis Fancher, Adolph Treidler, Frank Leyendecker of Arrow shirt fame, and others. These ads were quite appealing to those who could afford the best and wanted everyone to know it. Many originals of these paintings, which are now sought after as collectors' items, now reside at the University of Michigan Transportation Library.

The New York advertising firm of Collins and Holden was a pioneer in using the art form for automobile advertising. The Pierce Company utilized much of that firm's material. During Pierce-Arrow's golden years, the ten years before World War I, the expensive sales brochures were lovely works of art with many colored pictures (when you have it, flaunt it!). The plain sales pamphlets published in the mid-1930s reflected the sad financial state into which Pierce-Arrow had fallen.

From 1900 to 1904 the Pierce Company's production changed from bicycles to primarily automobiles, although it continued to make bicycles for some ten years more. The one-cylinder buggy was transformed into a powerful and reliable five-passenger touring car. It was to set the standard for the industry in years to come, and was on its way to becoming one of the most prestigious cars in America in the Edwardian age of elegance. Oldsmobile was producing more than 6,000 cars a year. Rolls and Royce hadn't yet made their Silver Ghost (1907). Packard and Peerless were destined to make quality cars also, but few manufacturers made a car to equal the Pierce Great Arrow.

Top—A 1901 Motorette from a Pierce sales brochure. Car number is A-7. (Courtesy of Dr. E.S.P. Cope.)
Bottom—The first Pierce Motorette (Model A), 1901, with a 2¾-horsepower, one-cylinder DeDion engine.
(From *The Story of Pierce-Arrow*—a 1930 Pierce-Arrow publication.)

The 1901 "Runabout" (3½-horsepower) and "Knockabout" (2¾-horsepower), which were entrants in the "New York to Buffalo Endurance Contest." The cars shown were A-8 and A-7. (Courtesy of the Motor Vehicle Manufacturers Association.)

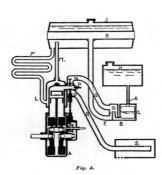

Fig. 4.

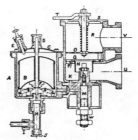

Fig. 5.—Longuemare Carburetter, modified to G. N. Pierce Company's requirements.

Fig. 4 is a diagram showing the motor and the arrangement of its various adjuncts, the names of which are as follows :

A—Motor.
B—Vaporizer.
C—Float chamber of vaporizer.
D—Mixing chamber of vaporizer.
E—Float needle valve of vaporizer.
F—Air inlet to vaporizer taking warm air from tube in water tank.
G—Mixed gas and air pipe from vaporizer to motor.
H—Gasoline tank.
J—Water tank for cooling cylinder.
K—Air pipe to cool water.
L—Cold water inlet pipe to cylinder.
M—Return water pipe from cylinder.
N—Inlet valve.
O—Exhaust valve.
P—Spark plug.
R—Exhaust pipe.
S—Exhaust silencer leading to atmosphere.
T—Radiating coil.

A—Body of constant level tank.
B—Float.
C—Cover of constant level tank.
D—Dust cap.
E—Spring Piston for depressing float.
F—Gasoline regulator needle-valve.
G—Balance levers.
H—Conical filter coupling.
I—Conical coupling for gasoline supply pipe.
J—Cleaning cap.
K—Air chamber.
L—Pulverizing spray plug.
M—Gasoline passage.
N—Strangling tube.
O—Perforated disc.
P—Direct passage for air.
Q—Mixture plate valve.
R—Gas chamber.
S—Cover for gas chamber.
T—Mixture plate lever.
U—Pure air inlet.
V—Explosive mixture outlet.
W—Stud support for carburetter.

Top—A Pierce publication showing the Motorette engine and Longuemare carburetor. *Bottom*—George Pierce in a 1902 Motorette in front of the Hanover Street factory with a Pierce bicycle in the background. (Courtesy of the Motor Vehicle Manufacturers Association.)

Top left and right—A 1903 Third Model Motorette (Model 5-FG) with and without the optional top. A 5-horsepower engine was used. The single wire armrest and center gas headlamp are characteristic of this model. (Courtesy of the Motor Vehicle Manufacturers Association.) *Center*—Circa 1903 Motorette. A man to be envied. (Courtesy of Phil Fisher.) *Bottom*—A 1903 Stanhope, Fourth Model (6-6½ H.K.), with a 6½-horsepower Pierce-made engine. (Courtesy of the Motor Vehicle Manufacturers Association.)

The 8-horsepower Stanhope of 1904 showing variations in available tops. The coupe top is actually shown on a late 1903 model (tiller instead of a steering wheel). The leather top with padded lining was $50 extra. (Courtesy of the Motor Vehicle Manufacturers Association.)

Although the fold-out front seat allowed for two additional passengers, their presence blocked the view of the driver. The extra weight in the front also made steering difficult. This led to the conventional French Panhard style of placing the engine in front, with the passenger seat behind the driver.

Top—A 1905 advertisement showing a Seventh Model (8-M) Stanhope. Note that most of the information is technical data. (Courtesy of the Pierce-Arrow Society.) *Bottom*—A 1903 Sixth Model Arrow (15-J) with a 15-horsepower, two-cylinder DeDion engine. The Renault-style hood has seven louvers on the side. (Courtesy of the Motor Vehicle Manufacturers Association.)

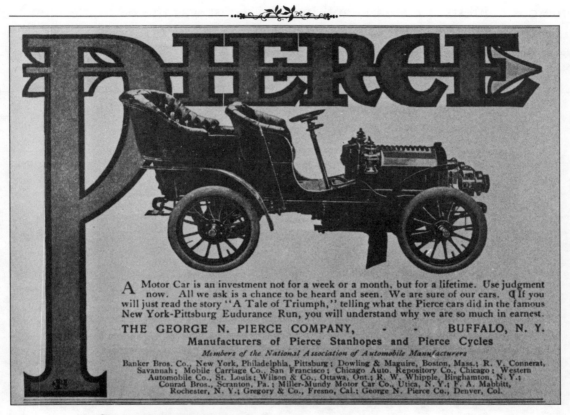

Top—This advertisement shows a late 1904 Arrow (Eighth Model). The hood (with fourteen louvers) and radiator have a more rounded top, characteristic of the later Pierce-Arrows. This is a transition between the 15-J and the Great Arrow (24-28N). (Courtesy of the Pierce-Arrow Society.) *Bottom*—A 1904 Eighth Model Arrow (15-J) with a 15-horsepower, two-cylinder Pierce engine. This uses a square Whitlock radiator and a square hood with fourteen louvers. (Courtesy of the Motor Vehicle Manufacturers Association.)

In the first decade of automobile building the Pierce Company entered and won numerous contests. One early and important test was the 800-mile New York to Pittsburgh Endurance Test, which started October 7, 1903, and ran for eight days. It was a week of heavy rains and fog. This was a grueling event over washed-out roads. Only twenty of the thirty-four entrants finished the race.

Percy Pierce and George Ulrich in an 8-horsepower Stanhope during the "New York to Pittsburgh Endurance Run," October 1903. (Courtesy of the Pierce-Arrow Society.)

Top—A 1904 Great Arrow Ninth Model (24–28N) with a canopy top. This hood had sixteen louvers on the top and sides. The car was taking on the "Pierce" look. No running boards were present. (Courtesy of the Motor Vehicle Manufacturers Association.) *Bottom*—Charles Sheppy and Herman May in an Eighth Model 1904 Arrow in the "New York to Pittsburgh Endurance Run." (Courtesy of the Pierce-Arrow Society.)

Top—A 1904 Great Arrow with Percy Pierce at the wheel. The front fenders are typical for 1904. Note the pressed-steel frame and the hood with sixteen louvers. (Courtesy of the Motor Vehicle Manufacturers Association.) *Bottom*—The first annual tour of the American Automobile Association from Boston to Saint Louis (July 27–August 10, 1904). The first-class certificate was awarded to the 24–28-horsepower Great Arrow. The driver of car 12 is Percy Pierce, with Colonel Clifton alongside. (Courtesy of the Motor Vehicle Manufacturers Association.)

In this 1909 *Country Life* advertisement, there was no technical data, only snob appeal. The original Pierce watercolors are beautiful. (Courtesy of the Pierce-Arrow Society.)

The one-cylinder buggy was transformed into a powerful and reliable five-passenger touring car. It was to set the standard for the industry in years to come, and was on its way to becoming one of the most prestigious cars in America in the Edwardian age of elegance.

This and facing page: A Pierce publication showing the evolution of their product. Quite a change in seven years. (Courtesy of the Pierce-Arrow Society.)

Oldsmobile was producing more than 6,000 cars a year. Rolls and Royce hadn't yet made their Silver Ghost (1907). Packard and Pearless were destined to make quality cars also, but few manufacturers made a car to equal the Pierce Great Arrow.

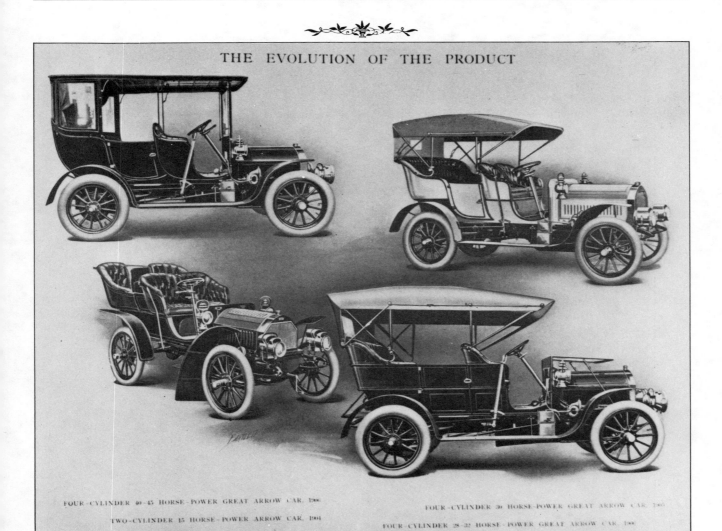

THE EVOLUTION OF THE PRODUCT

FOUR-CYLINDER 40-45 HORSE-POWER GREAT ARROW CAR. 1906

TWO-CYLINDER 15 HORSE-POWER ARROW CAR. 1904

FOUR-CYLINDER 30 HORSE-POWER GREAT ARROW CAR. 1905

FOUR-CYLINDER 28-32 HORSE-POWER GREAT ARROW CAR. 1904

PIERCE

THIS illustration shows the Pierce Great Arrow 28-32 Horse-Power Opera Coach, body by Quinby & Company. Price $5,000.

Great Arrow Enclosed Cars

THESE three types of enclosed cars have been built with a special thought for the user who expects the same perfection in the appointments of his automobile that he does in those of his carriages. These cars have the perfect mechanism of the Pierce cars, together with the most attractive and tasteful bodies ever turned out by Quinby. To appreciate their perfection they should be seen. We have been working steadily toward a very high standard in car-building, and believe now that the Pierce cars are American cars built by Americans for American conditions, American roads and the American temperament. Full descriptive booklet together with technical description of mechanisms will be mailed on request, or can be had of numerous Pierce agents all over the United States.

THIS illustration shows the Pierce Great Arrow 28-32 Horse-Power Suburban Car. Price $5,000.

THIS illustration shows the Pierce Great Arrow 28-32 Horse-Power Landaulet Car. Price $5,000.

The George N. Pierce Company, Buffalo, N. Y.

Manufacturers of Pierce Cycles.   Members of Association of Licensed Automobile Manufacturers.

$1,000 in Prizes

EVERY artist and designer should write at once for full particulars of our offer of prizes as follows : First prize of $250 and a second prize of $100 for the best design of an open body for a motor car ; first prize of $250 and a second prize of $100 for the best design of an enclosed or Limousine body for a motor car ; first prize of $200 and a second prize of $100 for the best color scheme for motor car bodies. Full description and outline drawings of Pierce cars will be supplied to artists for coloring.

3
STANDARDIZING THE LINE
1905–09

In 1873, George Brayton developed what was probably the best American gasoline engine of that time. An attorney, George Selden, applied for a patent on an automobile containing a Brayton engine in 1879 and laid the foundation for one of the biggest legal hassles in auto history. The Electric Vehicle Company of New York bought the patent for $10,000. Then forming the Association of Licensed Automobile Manufacturers (A.L.A.M.), on March 5, 1903, it subsequently filed suit against five auto manufacturers for not paying royalties on the automobiles that these manufacturers had produced. The George N. Pierce Company had joined the A.L.A.M. and paid its royalties. Colonel Clifton was one of the early presidents of the A.L.A.M.

Suit was filed against Henry Ford in 1903. The legal battle went on for eight years before Ford won the suit, breaking the hold of the Selden patent over all auto manufacturers. As an outgrowth of this legal battle, the Motor Vehicle Manufacturers Association was eventually formed to standardize and bring harmony to the new industry.

In 1904 the Pierce Company's production had consisted of three rather different types of automobile; the Stanhope, the Arrow, and the Great Arrow. Already work had begun on developing a big six-cylinder engine. George Pierce, now fifty-nine and in failing health, was becoming less active in the management

of his company. Birge, Clifton, May, and Fergusson were actually running the company, and doing it quite well. The company's slogan, "Pride of its makers makes you proud in possession," was more than a catchy phrase; it reflected the character of the founders. In 1905 the Society of Automotive Engineers was formed, and standardization was coming. In that year the Pierce Company was concentrating on the Great Arrow model, which was to become the mainstay of its line. The Stanhope continued unchanged in 1905 and went out of production in 1906. The Arrow Model (15-J) was also discontinued in 1905.

The Great Arrow was one of the largest and finest cars produced in America in 1905. It came in three models with four-cylinder engines of different horsepowers (24, 30, and 40 horsepower). The body was changed to a side-entrance tonneau with rear doors; there were no front doors.

The four-cylinder engine was a "T" head with individually cast cylinders. The oil pan and crankcase were of cast aluminum. The transmission employed ball bearings, slideshaft, and a bevel-gear drive. The gear-change lever was on the steering column. The tire size was 34 inches x 4 inches. The copper fuel tank, beneath the driver's seat, held 18 gallons. This gave a driving range of nearly 200 miles at 10 to 12 miles per gallon.

The "flood system" of lubrication used a two-gear

pump located in the well of the oil pan, which forced the oil up to an overhead reservoir. From there, three copper tubes carried the oil to the crankshaft bearings. "Mist" oiling was used for the cylinder and pistons. Fergusson was convinced that this was a superior system.

An additional feature this year was an "engine governor," in which the speed lever acted on the governor spring, which, in turn, acted on the throttle plate. By means of this control, the speed of the car was maintained at a predetermined speed, between 6 and 40 miles per hour, as set by the speed control lever. This, in effect, was a rudimentary "cruise control."

1905 Models
Model 24-28N
This 1905 Model 24-28N was essentially the same as the 1904 Great Arrow, with a canopy top. It had the same four-cylinder engine ($3^{15}/_{16}$ inch x $4^3/_4$ inch) as in 1904. The fender shape was changed, and a running board was added. The body style was the "King of Belgians" side-entrance tonneau with canopy, cape or Victoria tops available. The wheelbase increased to 100 inches and the weight to 2,500 pounds. The price without the top was $3,500, some $500 less than in 1904. All of the 1905 Great Arrow radiator shells had a characteristic scallop, similar to the Packard radiator of that year and different from other years. The body color was blue, with red running gear. The louvers on top of the hood were omitted in 1905, a distinguishing feature. The headlights were acetylene, and side lights were oil. Seventy-five of these small horsepower models were produced, but none survives.

Model 28–32NN
This model, new in 1905, had the larger four-cylinder engine (4½ inch x 4¾ inch) and was a popular model; 200 units were made. It was available in four body styles: the King of Belgians tonneau (104-inch wheelbase); Landaulet (109-inch wheelbase); Suburban (109-inch wheelbase), and Opera Coach (109-inch wheelbase). The bodies were all of cast aluminum and the last three styles were enclosed cars, with bodies by Quimby and Company. It is interesting to note that Pierce was leaning toward enclosed cars at a time when the overwhelming majority of cars being produced were open. The tastes of the "carriage trade"

may well have influenced this direction in styling.

The Opera Coach was the only rear-entrance vehicle, and all of the enclosed cars were intended to be chauffeur-driven. Aside from the King of Belgians, which was Quaker green with red running gear, color was optional on the other styles. The price ranged from $4,000 to $5,000. The Pierce-Arrow Society lists one of the 28-32NN King of Belgians models surviving in the Long Island Auto Museum.

Model 40-P
The largest engine produced in 1905 was the 40-horsepower, four-cylinder, 4⅞ inch x 5 inch. This was available in the same body styles as the 28-32NN. This model weighed 3,000 pounds, and only twenty-five were made.

Characteristics of this 1905 model year were rounded fenders, external brake, steering column gear lever, oil side lamps, drum headlamps, side-louvered hood, and scalloped radiator shell. By 1905, Pierce was already making one of the largest, best, and highest-priced cars in the United States.

The Big Six
The development of the automobile had advanced further in Europe than in America. During the summer of 1905, May and Fergusson toured Europe, visiting auto manufacturers to glean information. As a result, they decided to use the low-tension magneto patented in England by Mr. Critchley. They also ordered ball-bearings from Hess-Bright Manufacturing Company of Berlin for use in their 1906 transmission. The trend of Europe to adopt the six-cylinder engine showed Pierce management the wisdom of their decision to produce a six-cylinder engine.

Although development of a six-cylinder engine was begun in 1905, it was not until the summer of 1906 that testing began. An experimental six-cylinder Pierce car accompanied the 1906 Glidden Tour entrants.

This engine was to generate 60 horsepower with a bore and stroke of 5 inches by 5½ inches. The six-cylinder design promised smoothness and power, and the "big six" did not disappoint its developers. The six had less vibration, weighed less, and had faster acceleration. The production of 100 engines was begun in 1906, but they did not appear in the automobiles until the 1907 model in late 1906.

1906 Models: 28-32NN and 40-45PP

This year the small 24-28N and Stanhope models were dropped, and production was concentrated on the 28-32NN and 40-45PP models. A company publication lists the Stanhope as still available in 1906, but it is doubtful whether many, if any, were actually produced that late. By then it was rather out of style. The engine displacement was increased slightly from the previous year and available body styles were essentially the same as before, with a straight tonneau body, the Victoria tonneau body, Opera Coach, Suburban, and Landaulette. In addition, extra revolving seats were available in the 40-45PP model so that seven people could be accommodated (a new feature this year). Dust covers over leather seats were available at $50. The dual ignition used a jump spark and an autocoil. The sliding-gear transmission had three forward speeds and one reverse. Another new feature was a gasoline gauge mounted in the tank. The 28-32NN regularly came in dark blue with light blue striping, and the 40-45PP was dark Brewster green with light green striping. Other features were two side oil lamps, gas headlamps with gas generator, odometer and four shock absorbers. The side hood louvers were omitted this year. The radiator shell, scalloped in 1905, reverted to the typical Pierce shape. Tire size was 34 x 4 on smaller styles and 36 x 5 on larger cars. Goodrich tires were standard, with Michelin available at $100 extra. The 40-45PP weighed 3,100 pounds. Prices were increased by about $1,000 to $6,250—a very significant sum in 1906. There was no confusion about the clientele for whom these models were designed.

During this year 400 of the 28-32NN and 300 of the 45PP were manufactured. This was a respectable number, despite Oldsmobile's turning out nearly ten times that amount in 1905. Only two 1906 touring automobiles are known to survive.

The Glidden Trophy

During this period, the high cost of the Great Arrow and its reputation were not without some justification. The Pierce Great Arrow won the Glidden trophy in the first five years of the contest (1905, 1906, 1907, 1908, and 1909). The Glidden contest, which was held annually until 1913, was a good way of testing the reliability of the early automobiles, and a way of garnering free publicity.

Charles J. Glidden (1857–1927) was an enterprising businessman, who by 1900 had become a millionaire and had retired from the business that eventually became Bell Telephone. He was an avid automobile enthusiast and in 1901 began a tour around the world in his Napier that took seven years. He was instrumental in organizing an endurance run from New York to Saint Louis in 1904, under the auspices of the American Automobile Association. There was no prize offered in 1904, but the next year he donated the Glidden trophy. The trophy stood 50 inches high, was 18 inches in diameter of 400 ounces of sterling silver. It was to be awarded to the most roadworthy touring car in that 870-mile run from New York City to Bretton Woods, New Hampshire. Outperforming thirty-three cars, Percy Pierce won in his Great Arrow (28-32NN), receiving 996 points out of a possible 1,000. He was accompanied by his parents, his fiancée L. J. Moody, and his mechanic, George Ulrich. The eleven-day journey began in New York City and circled through New England. The trophy was presented to the Buffalo Auto Club, where it remained for several years; Percy received only pictures and medals. Also competing were Cadillac, Darracq, Locomobile, Napier, Packard, Panhard, and Peerless. The tale of the 1905 Glidden tour was recounted by Victor Speer in "Winning the Trophy."

In 1906, an expanded 1,134-mile Glidden run from Buffalo to New Hampshire, by way of Canada, was won by two Great Arrows and two Thomas Flyers. It ran from July 12 to July 28, 1906. Four Pierce automobiles were entered: Phillip Flynn of Pittsburgh drove a 28-32, (he also entered in 1907); Henry Paulman steered a 40-45; C. Henry Fosgate drove a 28-32 and Percy Pierce a 40-45. Ironically, just before the race the company did not have a car available for Percy, and he had to buy a car back from a recent purchaser in order to drive in the race. He won!

The 1907 Glidden tour, also known as the fourth annual AAA tour, ran from Cleveland to New York via Chicago, Indianapolis, Pittsburgh and Philadelphia. In the summer of 1907, a Pierce Great Arrow Pathfinder car drove the 1,470-mile course to lay out the route for the tour. Four Great Arrows finished with perfect scores; two of these were on the team which won the Glidden trophy for the Automobile Club of Buffalo. The story of the race appeared in a publication in 1907 as "Defending the Trophy" by

John Sullivan. The Chicago Motor Club held an economy run in September 1907 and a 30-horsepower Pierce Great Arrow averaged 20.6 miles per gallon, and that car weighed 4,545 pounds! Later that year, a 40-horsepower Pierce averaged 16.2 miles per gallon over 200 miles of bad road. Those were the good old days before pollution control.

The 1908 tour was from Buffalo to Saratoga Springs, New York. Three Pierce 60-horsepower cars entered and had perfect scores to win the trophy as a team. W. S. Winchester won the 1909 contest in his Pierce-Arrow and smaller Pierce runabouts won the Hower trophy in 1908 and 1909. The Great Arrows won almost every event they entered, which discouraged some makes from participating in contests against a Pierce car. The publicity did much to promote the reputation and the sales of the Great Arrow. In some of those early years, the anticipated production of the Pierce Company often was sold before the year began—an enviable position that unfortunately did not last beyond World War I. During those opulent Edwardian years the Pierce Arrow was one of "the best," and everyone knew it.

Expansion of Facilities
With the increase in production, (25 cars in 1901; 700 cars in 1905), the cramped facilities of the Hanover Street plant in 75,000 square feet became inadequate. On April 26, 1906, the 16-acre plot of land that had been the site of the 1901 Pan-American Exposition was purchased by the George Pierce Company to build their new Elmwood Plant with 331,460 square feet of floor space. The factory was completed on September 1, 1906. By 1916 the plant area had been increased to 1,500,000 square feet, on 44 acres. The plant was ultramodern, and the facilities and labor-management relations set a standard for the industry. The facility contained its own laboratory, hospital and cafeteria. The employees were fortunate to have working conditions better than most in the automobile industry. The employees of the Pierce plant had an "esprit de corps" rarely found in industry. In 1975 the old Elmwood Pierce-Arrow Motor Car Company building was dedicated as a National Historical Site.

Shortly after the completion of this building, Percy Pierce left the automobile business and in 1907 became head of the Pierce Cycle Company, which continued to build bicycles and motorcycles at the old Hanover Street plant. Henceforth, all automobile fabrication was to be at the new Elmwood Plant.

In 1909 the production of motorcycles was begun, which continued until about 1914. After bankruptcy, the Pierce bicycle business was sold to the Emblem Manufacturing Company, in Angola, N.Y.

Unlike the current yearly models, production of a model usually ran from one summer until the following summer: i.e., a "1906 model" was made from mid-1905 through mid-1906. Sometimes models ran longer, or new models were introduced in mid-season. As a result there is considerable confusion as to what was a 1907, 1908, 1909, or 1910 model, or what was characteristic of a particular year. Even Pierce-published data appears to be contradictory. The following will try to clarify these models and when they appeared.

1907–8
30-NN and 45-PP
In 1907 the two models of the previous year were continued as the 30-NN and the 45-PP. They were similar to but larger than the 1906 models. The respective wheelbases were increased to 112 inches and 124 inches. The four-cylinder 45-PP engine's bore and stroke remained at 5 inches x 5½ inches. The smaller model had a five-passenger side-entrance touring body, while the large 45-PP had a seven-passenger touring body with two extra revolving "jump" seats. The enclosed Suburban body was available with both sizes of chassis. This was also the year that the magneto first made its appearance, with two spark plugs for each cylinder. Colors were optional on all models. Prices were: Small Touring, $4,000; Small Suburban, $5,000; Large Touring, $5,000; Large Suburban, $6,250. The Cape Top was $200 extra. Only three 45-PP touring cars remain of 400 30-NN and 500 45-PP cars made.

Model 65-Q
The big event of 1907 was the introduction of the six-cylinder 65-horsepower engine (5 inches x 5½ inches) with six individually cast cylinders and seven main bearings for the crankshaft. The engine was powerful, smooth and quiet. The air-cooled Franklin had a six-cylinder engine also, but nevertheless Pierce was a pioneer in the multicylinder field. Unfortunately,

other manufacturers went on to eight-, twelve-, and sixteen-cylinder engines while Pierce stubbornly held onto its six. Although the engine remained a good one, the company could not dictate to the taste of the buying public. This conservatism was probably the first step in falling behind the other luxury car manufacturers.

The 65-Q Great Arrow of 1907 was made in the seven-passenger touring style, with folding seats. A Suburban body was also available. The wheelbase was stretched to a huge 135 inches, and the weight was 4,150 pounds. The gearshift was on the steering column; it had a reverse and three forward gears. Fabric seat covers were available. The touring body lines were smoother, and double moldings were used around the top of the body sides. The price, with top, for this "king of the road" was $6,500 and $7,750 for the Suburban. Only 166 were produced; one touring car survives.

A company publication dated November 1907 lists for 1907–8 a six-cylinder 40-horsepower (4¼ inches x 3¾ inches) tonneau. This was a midyear model (40-S) and could be considered a 1908 car, along with the other 30-NN, 45-PP, and 65-Q models made in 1908. This car had a 130-inch wheelbase and sold for $5,500 and, with the Suburban body, at $6,750. This model was between the 45-PP and 65-Q. The 1918 Pierce Recension Table lists this as a 1908 model 40-S. Although it was a midyear model, 352 were turned out. Actually, all of these 1907 models were made well into 1908, so that 1907 and 1908 models are the same, with the 40-S model being a 1908 issue.

The 1907–8 Great Arrows can be recognized by the rounded fenders and gearshift still mounted on the steering column; only the hand brake was outboard. The 1908 model 40-S had the newer "ski tip" rear fenders and square side lamps typical of 1909 models. The 40-S was later available in a three-seat runabout and a 4-seat tonneau. Company information states that the runabout style was introduced in 1909. Model years were not nearly as defined and rigid as they are today.

The 1909 models were brought out in September 1908. Some are pictured and titled as 1908 cars, although they have 1909 model characteristics.

1908 in the Industry

By 1908, 502 new automobile companies had been started—and 302 had already failed. The battle was to outproduce and outsell the competition. In 1908 Buick was producing 8,400 cars a year, and along with Oldsmobile had joined the newly formed General Motors Corporation. Cadillac was taken into the fold in 1909. By 1908 Henry Ford was producing his Model T, which sold for $850, while a Sears could be purchased for $395. Also in 1908 nonskid treads appeared on tires, and Fisher Body began building custom bodies.

1909

In his later years George Pierce was not the energetic and devoted worker that he had been earlier. He spent more time playing cards than with the automobile business. Fortunately May, Clifton, and Birge were aggressive managers, and they ran the company. With his health continuing to fail, George Pierce retired in 1909 to spend much of his time in Texas. He died of heart disease on May 23, 1910, at the Lenox Hotel in Buffalo. George K. Birge became president of the George N. Pierce Company in 1909 and continued to guide the company until he retired in 1916. Colonel Clifton was still treasurer; he was a strong influence in managing the company and very effective in directing the company's sales philosophy towards the "carriage trade" clientele. Henry May continued as vice president. His were the brains that ran the plant. In late 1908 the company name was changed to Pierce-Arrow Motor Car Company, and from then on the Great Arrow car was known as the Pierce-Arrow. Thus, Great Arrow refers only to cars made between 1904 and 1908.

The logo of the arrow, with the superimposed script "Pierce," had been used by the company on early bicycles and in advertising and later became an option on the front of the automobile radiator.

The year 1909 saw motorized vehicles in service at the White House, replacing the horse-drawn carriages. President William Howard Taft was the first president to use the automobile officially. George H. Robinson, President Taft's chauffeur, was responsible for selecting the first fleet of cars for government use at the White House. He ordered a 1909 Pierce-Arrow Landaulette, a 1909 Pierce-Arrow Brougham, a Baker Electric and a White Steamer. These all arrived in time for President Taft's inauguration in January 1909. How long these Pierce-Arrows were used and their final disposition is not known. Taft himself later owned a 1912 Pierce-Arrow 66-QQ. As far as the Pierce-Arrow Society knows, none of these three Pierce-Arrows exists today.

Something for Everyone

The retirement of George Pierce in 1909 and the withdrawal of Percy Pierce from auto manufacturing in 1907 may have unfettered the company's goals. Or perhaps it was the expanded facilities or the state of the science. At any rate, the number of 1909 models (actually late 1908 and 1909) proliferated greatly, as seen in the table below.

This was the last year of the four-cylinder engine except in trucks. Interestingly, the engine cylinders were made either as pairs or cast singly. The 30-U model was experimental; only three units were made. Of the nearly 1,000 cars built by Pierce-Arrow in 1909, the writer knows of five survivors. In that same year Ford turned out some 18,000 Model T cars!

Besides six different chassis, several new body styles were available, including the two- or three-passenger Runabout on the 24 or 36-horsepower chassis (called a touring car on the larger chassis) and a five-passenger Landaulet on the 24- and 36-horsepower chassis. The larger seven-passenger Landau was available on the three larger chassis. The five-passenger Brougham on the smaller chassis corresponded to the seven-passenger Suburban on the larger chassis. Touring cars came with three, four, five, six or seven seats. On the small, enclosed cars the extension top and sliding glass front were $400 extra. Prices for thirty-one styles ranged from $3,050 to $7,200.

The ignition had two separate systems; individual jump spark units and a high-tension magneto. The transmission in 1909 had *four* forward speeds. Colors were optional, as usual, but all of the chassis were painted lead gray. The fenders were still rounded except on the smaller touring cars, which had sloping front fenders. In 1910, all of the models had the sloping front fenders. The rear fenders were the "ski tip" type found on the 1908 model 40-S. In late 1908 and 1909 the gearshift lever was moved from the steering column to the "outboard" position with the hand brake. Also, there was no splash pan between the running board and frame as was found on the 1910 models.

Quality Control

The Great Arrow's successful performance was largely due to the company's high standards of manufacturing and inspection. Engines were tested with dynamometers, then torn down, inspected, reassembled and rerun. The engine was mounted on the chassis for a hundred-mile road test. Only then was the body placed on the chassis and a final road test carried out to check the performance and noise. A smooth and quiet engine was of the utmost importance. Cast aluminum bodies and helical gears were two big factors contributing to a quiet performance.

As was standard practice in Europe, the Pierce-Arrow Company offered two-week training courses for chauffeurs, garage mechanics, and dealers for instruction on the maintenance and operation of the six-cylinder Pierce automobiles. Attendance was possible through dealer recommendation.

End of a Decade

By the end of the first decade of automobile production by the George N. Pierce Company many changes had occurred. The "buggy" evolved into one of the largest, most expensive, and best built cars in America. The founder had died. Bicycle and motorcycle fabrication had split away from the automobile manufacturing. The company name had been changed to the Pierce-Arrow Motor Car Company. And although the firm had made tremendous progress, even better cars were yet to come.

1909 Models

Model	Cylinders	Bore and Stroke	Wheelbase	Tire	Approximate Number Produced
24-T	4 (pair)	$3^{15}/_{16}$ x 4¾	111½	36 x 4	103
36-UU	6 (pair)	$3^{15}/_{16}$ x 4¾	119	34 x 4	307
40-PP	4 (single)	5 x 5½	130	36 x 4	101
48-SS	6 (pair)	4½ x 4¾	130	36 x 4	359
60-QQ	6 (single)	5 x 5½	135	36 x 4½	83
30-U	6 (single)	3¾ x 3¾	125	34 x 4	3

Left top, center, and bottom—Shown in a 1905 catalog, the last model Stanhope and the Great Arrow with the canopy top and cape top. (Courtesy of the University of Michigan.) *Right top, center, and bottom*—The three enclosed body styles on the 1905 Great Arrow were Landaulet, Suburban, and Opera Coach. Note the scalloped radiator and hood with eighteen louvers used only in 1905. (Courtesy of the University of Michigan.)

PIERCE

THIS illustration shows the Pierce Great Arrow 28-32 Horse-Power Opera Coach, body by Quinby & Company. Price $5,000.

Great Arrow Enclosed Cars

THESE three types of enclosed cars have been built with a special thought for the user who expects the same perfection in the appointments of his automobile that he does in those of his carriages. These cars have the perfect mechanism of the Pierce cars, together with the most attractive and tasteful bodies ever turned out by Quinby. To appreciate their perfection they should be seen. We have been working steadily toward a very high standard in car-building, and believe now that the Pierce cars are American cars built by Americans for American conditions, American roads and the American temperament. Full descriptive booklet together with technical description of mechanisms will be mailed on request, or can be had of numerous Pierce agents all over the United States.

THIS illustration shows the Pierce Great Arrow 28-32 Horse-Power Suburban Car. Price $5,000.

THIS illustration shows the Pierce Great Arrow 28-32 Horse-Power Landaulet Car. Price $5,000.

The George N. Pierce Company, Buffalo, N. Y.

Manufacturers of Pierce Cycles.   Members of Association of Licensed Automobile Manufacturers.

$1,000 in Prizes

EVERY artist and designer should write at once for full particulars of our offer of prizes as follows : First prize of $250 and a second prize of $100 for the best design of an open body for a motor car ; first prize of $250 and a second prize of $100 for the best design of an enclosed or limousine body for a motor car ; first prize of $200 and a second prize of $100 for the best color scheme for motor car bodies. Full description and outline drawings of Pierce cars will be supplied to artists for coloring.

An advertisement from April 1905 *Country Life in America* showing the scalloped radiator shell. At the bottom, notice the contest, which was entered by Herbert Dawley. (Courtesy of the Pierce-Arrow Society.)

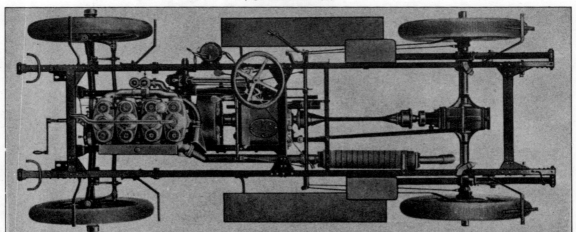

The 1906 chassis with engine that had four cylinders, cast singly. (Courtesy of the Motor Vehicle Manufacturers Association.)

The four body styles in the 1906 model: Cape-top Tonneau, canopy top on a Victoria Tonneau, Suburban, and Laudaulet. (Courtesy of the Pierce-Arrow Society.)

Top—The Glidden Trophy won by Pierce Great Arrows from 1905 through 1909. It was 50 inches tall, weighed 400 ounces, and was made of sterling silver. (Courtesy of the Motor Vehicle Manufacturers Association.) *Bottom*—The winner of the first Glidden Trophy Race (1905), the 28-horsepower Great Arrow. The driver is Percy Pierce with his father, George Pierce, seated behind him. (Courtesy of the Motor Vehicle Manufacturers Association.)

Top—The 1907 Pathfinder Great Arrow in Indianapolis, Indiana. The Pierce team is talking with the chief of police. (Courtesy of the Motor Vehicle Manufacturers Association.) *Bottom*—The 1907 Pathfinder going through Greenfield, Indiana, on old Route 40. "Which way to the car wash?" (Courtesy of the Motor Vehicle Manufacturers Association.)

Top—The start of the 1907 Glidden Tour, Cleveland, Ohio. Mr. P.S. Flynn, driving, and wife. (Courtesy of the Motor Vehicle Manufacturers Association.) *Bottom*—Entering the 1907 Glidden Trophy took much fortitude (being a little "crazy" helped too). (Courtesy of the Motor Vehicle Manufacturers Association.)

The Great Arrows won almost every event they entered, which discouraged some makes from participating in contests with a Pierce car. The publicity did much to promote the reputation and the sales of the Great Arrow. In some of those early years, the anticipated production of the Pierce Company often was sold before the year began—an enviable position that unfortunately did not last beyond World War I. During those opulent Edwardian years the Pierce-Arrow was one of "the best," and everyone knew it.

Top—Getting ready for the start of the 1908 Glidden Tour in Buffalo, New York. (Courtesy of the Motor Vehicle Manufacturers Association.) *Bottom*—A 1907 Model 30NN miniature tonneau (Engine #3369). Note earlier type front fenders similar to the 1904 style. (Courtesy of the University of Michigan.)

Top—A 1908 photograph showing the new Elmwood plant, begun in 1906. (Courtesy of the University of Michigan.) *Center and bottom*—A 1907 30NN Touring (with seat covers) and a 45PP Suburban. Front and rear fenders were rounded in 1907 and 1908. (Courtesy of the University of Michigan.)

Top—A late 1907 45PP Runabout (Engine #4507). The chief of the Saint Paul Fire Department
had taste. (Courtesy of the University of Michigan.) *Bottom*—The new six-cylinder engine introduced in the
1907 Model 65-Q. In 1908 it was also used in the 40-S chassis. The cylinders were cast singly.
(Courtesy of the University of Michigan.)

Top—Percy Pierce in a 1908 40-S Great Arrow in front of the Saint Louis Church, Buffalo, New York. (Courtesy of the Motor Vehicle Manufacturers Association.) *Bottom*—The New York Auto Show. The 1908 and 1909 style cars appear in the picture. (Courtesy of the Motor Vehicle Manufacturers Association.)

Top—"Roughing it" in a 1908 Great Arrow. (Courtesy of the Motor Vehicle Manufacturers Association.)
Bottom—The 1908 New York Auto Show with a 1909 Model Roadster in the background.
(Courtesy of the Motor Vehicle Manufacturers Association.)

Top—A 1908 Model 40-S Great Arrow with the new type "ski tip" rear fenders. (Courtesy of the University of Michigan.) *Bottom*—A 1908 Model 65-Q Touring Car. The tufted leather seats had seat covers. The larger models had rounded rear fenders. (Courtesy of the University of Michigan.)

Top—The luxurious 1908 40-S Suburban. The square side lamps were new starting in 1908.
(Courtesy of the University of Michigan.) *Bottom*—The 1908 40-S Landau. The last year for the steering-
wheel-mounted gear shift. (Courtesy of the University of Michigan.)

Two variations in top treatment for the four-passenger 40-S Touring. (Courtesy of the University of Michigan.)

Two- and three-seat Roadsters in 1908. Models 65-Q above and 40-S below.
(Courtesy of University of Michigan.)

A family picnic (1908) in a 40-S Great Arrow. (Courtesy of the University of Michigan.)

Above—A 1909 Model 36-UU, five-passenger Touring. *Below*—A 40-PP, seven-passenger Touring.
Starting with the 1909 Models, the gearshift was "outboard" with the parking brake.
(Courtesy of the University of Michigan.)
Facing page: *Top*—A 1909 Model 48-SS Touring car. (Courtesy of the University of Michigan.)
Center—A 1918 Series 5 car showing the optional script "Pierce." (Courtesy of the Pierce-Arrow Society.)
Bottom—The huge 60-QQ Touring car. (Courtesy of the University of Michigan.)

Top left and right—The 1909 small Landaulet was for town driving. This Model 24-T had only a four-cylinder engine. The front view shows how narrow the body was. (Courtesy of the University of Michigan.)
Bottom—The elegant (but dark) interior of the 1909 Landaulet. (Courtesy of the University of Michigan.)

Open views of the 1909 smaller Landaulet and larger Landau. Note the beautiful coach lamps.
(Courtesy of the University of Michigan.)

The 1909 Models 36-UU Brougham and 40-PP Suburban. Note that there is no splash pan between the frame and running board. (Courtesy of the University of Michigan.)

As was standard practice in Europe, the Pierce-Arrow Company offered two-week training courses for chauffeurs, garage mechanics, and dealers for instruction on the maintenance and operation of the six-cylinder Pierce automobiles. Attendance was possible through dealer recommendation.

The opulent interior of a 1909 Suburban. Note the special side lights. (Courtesy of the University of Michigan.)

Top—A factory publication showing two six-cylinder engines: one cast in pairs (Model 48-SS) and one cast singly (Model 60-QQ). (Courtesy of the Motor Vehicle Manufacturers Association.) *Bottom*—A view of the beautiful workmanship in the seven-passenger Touring. It has one revolving seat and one folding seat. (Courtesy of the University of Michigan.)

The interior of the cast-aluminum body showing riveted joints along with supports for the folding top.
(Courtesy of the University of Michigan.)

4
THE
SECOND DECADE—THE APOGEE
1910–13

By 1910 developments in the auto industry had progressed to speedometers, shock absorbers, foot accelerators, electric horns, compressed-air self-starters, gas lights, bumpers, and running boards, all commonly available on most cars. In 1910 the Society of Automotive Engineers instituted standardization in auto manufacturing. B. T. Carter, designer of the Carter car, died from backfire while cranking a Cadillac engine. Shocked by the death of his friend, Leland insisted that a self-starter be designed for Cadillac. A successful starter, designed by Charles Kettering, first appeared on the 1912 Cadillac, for which Kettering received the Dewar Cup from the R.A.C. in England.

By 1910 the Pierce-Arrow design had stabilized to the extent that there were now three basic chassis instead of the six available in 1909. The company apparently felt that these three chassis offered the best features of all the previous versions. The three standard chassis were the mainstay of its output for most of the coming decade. Except for trucks, first built in 1911, the engines were all six-cylinder, cast in pairs. Reducing the number of available chassis and engines led to economy in manufacturing. Changes in design in subsequent years were not major, but simply refined and improved the product. It was during this decade that the company produced some of its finest cars and was the industry's leader in quality—"the best car that money could build." The three models retained were

the 36-UU, 48-SS, and 66-QQ with those respective horsepowers.

1910
36-UU, 48-SS, 66-QQ

During the 1910 model year (actually between July 1909 and July 1910), about 1,530 automobiles were made. There were about 600 of the 36-UU, about 800 of the 48-SS and about 100 of the 66-QQ produced. Of these, eleven survive: four 36-UU; six 48-SS, and one 66-QQ. The respective bores and strokes of the engines were slightly larger at 4 x 4¾, 4½ x 4¾, and 5¼ x 5½. All chassis had a four-speed gearbox with the hand gear-change lever still outboard, along with the brake lever. The chassis were essentially the same as the corresponding ones of the 1908–9 models.

The body styles ranged from the 119-inch wheelbase Runabout (the affluent gentleman must have his plaything), at $3,850 to the 134½-inch wheelbase Landau at $7,200. Also available were the four, five or seven-passenger touring cars with 125-inch, 134½-inch, and 140-inch wheelbase, Brougham (125-inch wheelbase), Suburban (134½-inch wheelbase), Landaulet (125-inch wheelbase), and Landau (134½-inch wheelbase). The wheelbases were lengthened about five inches over the previous models. Wheel sizes varied from 36 x 4 to 38 x 5½.

In this year the power air pump, which was driven

by a take-off from the transmission and could be used for pumping up tires, became available. This accessory was used for the next fifteen years. Also new this year was the priming pump. The double body molding of the 1909 touring cars was replaced by a single molding. This, plus the new splash pan between the running boards and the body, gave cleaner lines in 1910. The hood and cowl lines were less disjointed, also. The horn bulb was on the floor by the driver's foot, while in 1911 this was moved outside the body (a differentiating feature). All 1910 models had sloping front fenders. Interestingly, closed models had different style headlamps from the touring cars. With the 1910 cars, Pierce-Arrow was beginning to reach its stride in producing a refined automobile. About 1,500 cars were produced that year.

Birge's Special Touring Landau (1910)
George Birge, then president of Pierce-Arrow, was a gentleman of the arts and a world traveler. In 1910 a very special model was made for Mr. Birge. Herbert Dawley helped in the design. This was a special touring Landau on a 66-QQ chassis, first exhibited at the Madison Square Garden Show. Since travel by automobile, and the facilities available for the traveler, were trying at best, this forerunner of the motor home was designed to give the early motorist some extra comforts. The standard deck over the chauffeur's seat was replaced by a folding Victoria top for increased visibility in fair weather. The running boards were enlarged to contain storage compartments. There was a sliding drawer under the rear seat, and the rear trunk was greatly enlarged. The back of the chauffeur's seat contained a fold-out water basin supplied with running water from a pressurized tank beneath the body. This ultimate vehicle for extended touring could be owned for $8,250. At least three of these behemothic vehicles were made (Mr. Post of cereal fame owned one), and their whereabouts are unknown.

1911
36-UU, 48-SS, 66-QQ
Except for minor variations, 1911 was a repeat of 1910 with the three standard chassis (36-UU, 48-SS and 66-QQ). The bore and stroke was increased slightly to 4 x 5⅛, 4½ x 5½ and 5¼ x 5½ respectively. Body styles were again similar, with three, four, five and seven-passenger touring (the 66-QQ having a 140-

inch wheelbase), plus Brougham, Suburban, Landaulet, and Landau. A new model this year was the "protected touring car," which had detachable front doors. A vented windshield was used on this car to cool the people in the front seat. The enclosed body styles had front half-doors. The addition of front doors was really the only major change in 1911. Prices again ranged from $3,850 to $7,200. Approximately 1,000 of the 36-UU and 48-SS cars were made, while only 200 of the large 66-QQ were built. About eleven cars survive from 1911.

1912
36-UU, 48-SS, 66-QQ
Again, there was little basic change in the three standard models. The same body styles (Runabout, assorted tourings, Brougham, Suburban, Landaulet and Landau) were built on the three basic chassis (36-UU, 48-SS, and 66-QQ). The 1910 through 1912 models mainly saw refinement of a basically well-designed automobile with small increases in engine displacement and wheelbase. Production was increased to about 3,000 cars that year. Front doors were now standard on all 1912 models, and the gearshift and brake levers were brought inboard. The double molding was again back on the touring bodies, and the strips were close together near the top of the body. A major difference in the enclosed styles was the arched roof over the rear doors. This characteristic design persisted for several years. However, the straight-top door was still available as an option. Rear fenders were more rounded with a trailing flange, and the splash pans were larger to cover all of the frame. The oil side lamps had a new chimney design in 1912. Although the head lamps were still acetylene, the dash lights were electric. Along with the electric horn, this was the first step towards a complete electrical system. This year a movable split windshield was available for ventilation, made necessary by the presence of front doors.

Standard equipment on all 1912 models included:
Two Prest-O-Lite gas head lamps
Two dash and one rear combination oil and electric lamps
One rear number electric lamp
Horn and full set of tools
Folding glass front
Power air pump
Gasoline tank air pressure gauge on dash

Odometer
Four shock absorbers
Extra tire carrier and trunk rack
Gasoline primer for easy starting
Yale locks throughout the car
Demountable tire rims (Johnson Patent)

The ignition had two separate systems: jump spark with one master vibrator and a Bosch high-tension magneto.

Because of the large bore and stroke (5 x 7) on the 66-QQ, the maximum engine rpm was only 1,400. Prices this year ranged from $3,250 to $7,100. This was far beyond the means of the average workman making $50 per week. Car colors were optional, generally in one or two colors. The mixing of warm and cool colors was suggested by the company art department. Interiors were luxurious, and generally specified by the customer. Considerable time and effort was spent by the buyer with the design department, not unlike designing a house. Herbert Dawley planned the details of the car for the requirements and tastes of the buyer.

1913 (Series One)
38-C, 48-B, 66-A

In 1913 the same basic body styles and similar chassis were available. The horsepowers were 38, 48, and 66 with the respective wheelbases increased to 132 inches, 142 inches, and 147½ inches. Beginning in 1913 the production was designated as a series (Series One). The four succeeding series continued into 1919. The three models in this first series were 38-C-1, 48-B-1, and 66-A-1.

In addition to the standard models, a low-production model, 48-D, was available in a seven-passenger touring car on a small 134½-inch wheelbase. A standard 48 horsepower engine, and a price of $5,000 filled a gap between the 38-C-1 and 48-B-1. Only 134 cars of this 48-D were built.

Two new styles were introduced in 1913 in the 147½-inch chassis, the vestibule Suburban and vestibule Landau. In these, the chauffeur's compartment was completely enclosed and had doors with glass windows. These styles remained through Series Five cars.

The new features of the 1913 Series One cars were the compressed air starter and the complete electrical system, including headlights and Klaxon horn. Cadillac had an electric starter in 1912, but Pierce did not utilize one until the Series Two cars in the summer of 1913. Compressed air starters first appeared in the auto industry about 1909.

A distinguishing feature in 1913 cars was a conical electric head lamp replacing the drum gas lamps of 1912. Also, the front fenders had a double curve rather than the straight, sloping lines of 1912. The radiator shell was frequently painted to match the body color. Many radiator shells were nickel-plated, but some were left brass even though other parts were nickel.

The compressed-air starter was standard equipment. A four-cylinder air pump driven by a transmission-powered take-off was standard. This made compressed air available to inflate the tires and start the engine the next time. The six-cylinder engine, cast in pairs, is shown in the illustration.

Actually, three basic chassis continued from 1912 through 1918 with only relatively minor changes. The management had a good design, and with its prestigious position in the market established, felt little pressure to make radical changes. Emphasis on truck production during the war years also slowed progress in design. One significant change in the Pierce-Arrow was coming soon: fender-mounted front headlamps, suggested by the young Pierce-Arrow designer, Herbert Dawley. This feature was to become the trademark of future Pierce-Arrows, beginning with the model 48-B-2 introduced in May 1913.

Herbert M. Dawley (1880–1970)

Herbert Dawley was born in Chillicothe, Ohio, in March 1880. His association with the Pierce Company began in 1906, when the company held a design contest. The entries were judged by "men of prominence," and prizes were awarded. The Pierce directors liked the work submitted by Dawlay, though the judges did not award him a prize. He was offered a position in the Pierce Company in 1907 under Birge and Colonel Clifton, with whom he developed very close ties. Although Dawley's education was in mechanical engineering, he functioned in the company areas of art, design, sales and customer relations, later as head of the Art Department. He was soon in a position to associate with many important people within and outside the company.

One of his early contributions to the Pierce car was

standardizing the hardware by using the hexagon motif, as seen on the hubcaps. In 1912 Colonel Clifton asked him to come up with a design for the Pierce which would be distinctive and unique. His idea for a fender headlight meant better road illumination, because of its higher position than the drum headlight. Unique, it made the Pierce immediately recognizable. At first the idea was ridiculed by his associates, but the new fenders were put on Mr. Birge's car experimentally. Shortly afterwards, the innovation became available as an option. Because fender headlights were unique to the prestigious Pierce, it wasn't long before they became standard and the drum lights optional. This option of drum headlights lasted until about 1935, but Pierce cars with drum headlights are rather scarce today, especially on cars made after 1932. At least one 1938 Brunn Town Brougham with separate headlights was known to exist.

The two ideas contributed by Herbert Dawley have been incorporated into the emblem of the Pierce-Arrow Society. With World War I came changes in the company's management and philosophy, and at the end of 1917 Dawley left Pierce-Arrow. After serving in World War I as a major, he became an actor and spent most of his life as a theatrical director. But in ten years with Pierce-Arrow he had left a permanent mark.

Truly these were the halcyon years at Pierce-Arrow. Management was stable and unified. The company's image was established and enviable. The market was solid. Their product was magnificent, and these are now the most sought-after models by collectors.

The 1910 Model 36-UU Miniature Tonneau and Touring cars, with the added splash pan between the running boards and the frame characteristic of this year. (Courtesy of the University of Michigan.)

Top—A 1910 Model 48-SS Victoria Runabout. (Courtesy of the University of Michigan.)
Center—The huge 1910, 66-QQ, seven-passenger Touring. The large chassis usually carried Touring-type bodies for out-of-town traveling. (Courtesy of the University of Michigan.) *Bottom*—The front end of an enclosed 1910 automobile, using a different style of side lamp. (Courtesy of the University of Michigan.)

Top—Two views of the 1910 six-cylinder engine. The engines were all cast in pairs from 1910 on. (Courtesy of the University of Michigan.) *Bottom*—The bare 1910 chassis. (Courtesy of the University of Michigan.)

Top—A 1910 Model 36-UU Brougham. Town car type bodies were usually on smaller horsepower chassis. (Courtesy of the University of Michigan.) *Center*—A 1910 Model 48-SS Suburban. Note that the horn bulb is still on the floor (for the last year—a 1910 characteristic). (Courtesy of the University of Michigan.) *Bottom*—A 1910 Model 36-UU Landaulet. (Courtesy of the University of Michigan.)

Top—George Birge's special Touring Landau on a 1910 66-QQ chassis. (Courtesy of the University of Michigan.) *Center*—The interior of George Birge's Landau (even the kitchen sink). (Courtesy of the University of Michigan.) *Bottom*—Mr. Birge off for parts unknown. (Courtesy of the Motor Vehicle Manufacturers Association.)

Top—A 1910 Roadster. You'd look smug too if you owned one of these. (Courtesy of Dr. E. S. P. Cope.)
Center—A 1911 Model 36-UU Miniature Tonneau. The horn bulb was moved to the body side this year and is a
differentiating characteristic. (This photo was actually *retouched* from the corresponding 1910 picture.)
(Courtesy of the University of Michigan.) *Bottom*—A 1911 Model 48-SS "closed coupled" Touring.
(Courtesy of the University of Michigan.)

Top—A 1911 Model 48-SS Runabout, little changed from the corresponding 1910 model. (Courtesy of the University of Michigan.) *Center*—A 1911 Model 48-SS "protected" Touring. This was the first year and model with front doors. (Courtesy of the University of Michigan.) *Bottom*—A 1911 Model 66-QQ, seven-passenger Touring. (Courtesy of the University of Michigan.)

Top—A 1911 Model 48-SS Landau. This is similar to the 1910 model but with half doors added in front. (Courtesy of the University of Michigan.) *Bottom*—A Pierce-Arrow showroom, circa 1912. (Courtesy of the University of Michigan.)

A 1912 Model 36-UU Roadster and Touring. All models had front doors in 1912. Touring cars had double mouldings. (Courtesy of the University of Michigan.)

The 1912 Model 48-SS and 66-QQ Touring cars. Note the side lamps and rear fender design.
(Courtesy of the University of Michigan.)

A 1912 Model 36-UU Brougham and a 66-QQ Vestibule (enclosed front) Suburban.
(Courtesy of the University of Michigan.)

Top—A 1912 Model 36-UU Landaulet (elegant transportation). (Courtesy of the University of Michigan.)
Bottom—The dashboard of a restored 1912 36-UU Touring. (Owner: Fred Rouse.)

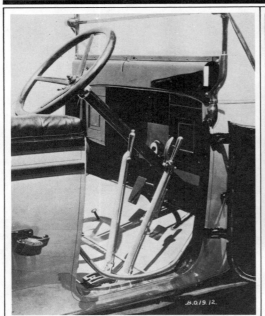

Top left and right—Details of the 1912 model. (Courtesy of the University of Michigan.)
Bottom—A 1913, 38-C Roadster. Starting with this series car, there were two ventilators on top of the hood.
(Courtesy of the University of Michigan.)

Top—A 1913, 48-B Touring. (Courtesy of the University of Michigan.) *Bottom*—A 1913, 48-B Touring with running board and mounted spare tires. (Courtesy of the University of Michigan.)

Top—A 1913, 66-A, seven-passenger Touring. The front bumpers were available but not standard. The 66-horsepower engine was the largest production engine ever made (*Guinness Book of World Records*). (Courtesy of the University of Michigan.) *Bottom*—A 1913, 38-C Landaulet with a painted radiator shell (optional). (Courtesy of the University of Michigan.)

Top—A 1913, 66-A Suburban with special railing about the roof. (Courtesy of the University of Michigan.)
Bottom—A view of the 1913 Series 1 instrument panel. (Courtesy of the University of Michigan.)

A Series 1 (1913) front end showing the new electrical headlamps with plain glass lenses.
(Courtesy of the University of Michigan.)

Top—The intake side of a Series 1 engine with dual spark plugs. (Courtesy of the University of Michigan.)
Center—The logo of the Pierce-Arrow Society utilizing two features typical of the Pierce-Arrow:
the fender headlights and the hexagon motif. (Courtesy of the Pierce-Arrow Society.)
Bottom—Herbert M. Dawley (1880–1970). He designed the fender-mounted headlamps. The patent was
applied for December 1912 and granted February 1914. (Courtesy of the Pierce-Arrow Society.)

5
THE
WAR YEARS
1914–19

The world was upon the threshold of a war in 1914. President Wilson advocated neutrality, but everyone was preparing for war production. At Pierce, automobile production was relatively de-emphasized, while military truck production witnessed a tremendous growth. In 1914 the French government ordered 600 trucks from Pierce, and 300 more in 1915. In England there was little domestic truck production; they looked to the United States to fill their needs. Ironically, of all the Pierce trucks used in England during World War I, only one could be found after World War II, surprising considering the British penchant toward husbandry. That remaining truck was restored for the film *The Blue Max*. By 1917, Pierce truck production outnumbered cars two to one. By 1918, this ratio was almost seven to one. These sales meant good financial years. The successful company was doing even better, but at the expense of automobile development and production.

The process of "thermal cracking" used in producing gasoline was developed just prior to the war, in 1913, to supply more and better gasoline at a time when it was needed. For several years there were no major changes in the Pierce-Arrow cars, although the engineering staff was experimenting on new and improved engines to garner more of the market.

Series Two (1914)

In 1914 the big change was the appearance of fender headlights on the production automobile. The design patent was applied for December 12, 1912, and Patent No. 25,290; Serial No. 738,076 was actually granted February 24, 1914, to Herbert Dawley. The model 48-B-2 was the first to carry this innovation. A separate, steel headlight was riveted to the fender, a feature synonymous with Pierce-Arrow during the remaining twenty-four years of production. Although somewhat strange-looking, it did identify the Pierce-Arrow owner. Quickly this option became the standard style, and fifty years later it is still the best-remembered characteristic of the Pierce-Arrow.

Factory photographs of the Series One through Series Five cars show plate-glass lenses in the headlights. Some states required fluted lenses to disperse the light. Consequently many people changed the lenses. Restorers now frequently put Bausch and Lomb fluted lenses in their cars. Either could therefore be considered correct. These Bausch and Lomb lenses were not originally tinted violet, but with long exposure to daylight, many have gradually turned that shade.

Also making its appearance in 1914 was the Westinghouse electric starter (replacing the old compressed-air starter) and generator. The starter was activated by a floor pedal. Along with the electric lights of Series One, the cars now had a complete electrical system.

The three basic chassis were the 38-C-2, 48-B-2, and 66-A-2. The available body styles were essentially the same as before. The vestibule Landau and Suburban were still on the huge 147½-inch-wheelbase 66-A-2 chassis. These elegant vehicles exemplified the craftsmanship that earned for Pierce-Arrow the appelation of the American Rolls-Royce. The cars made during this period (Series One through Series Five) were largely responsible for Pierce-Arrow's great reputation. Along with the rumblings of world war came many worldwide changes. Unfortunately the Pierce-Arrow Company didn't change with the times, and its cars became antiquated. The next twenty years would not be as kind to Pierce-Arrow as the past twenty.

The body lines on the Series Two cars were smoother. Front fenders were rounded again. Even then manufacturers seemed to change design simply for the sake of change. The sidelights were integrated with the cowl and stayed that way for the remaining three series. The mechanical specifications of the three chassis changed little throughout the series. Tire sizes ranged from 36 inches x 4½ inches to 38 inches x 5½ inches. (The larger size was on the rear wheels.) The three engines were changed little. The 66-horsepower engine had a 5 inch x 7 inch bore and stroke for 824 cubic inches. The *Guinness Book of World Records* lists this as the largest American production automobile engine ever made. Approximately 1,500 Series 2 cars were manufactured from May 1913 to July 1914. Even Pierce-Arrow tables vary in production figures.

Series Three (1915)

The Series Three, although a 1915 model, actually was produced from June 1914 to February 1916. The three basic chassis were again similar to previous years. Body styles, although like the Series Two cars, were more stylish and offered more variations. There were some new types: Roadster; Coupe Roadster and Coupe; four-five-seven passenger-Touring; Brougham; Landaulet; Sedan; Brougham-Landaulet; Vestibule-Brougham; Vestibule-Laundaulet; Vestibule-Brougham-Landaulet; Suburban; Landau; Vestibule-

Suburban; Vestibule Landau; and Vestibule-Suburban-Landau. Nearly sixty combinations were available. All touring cars were furnished with the "solitaire" top. The standard tire was the Goodrich Silvertown cord. All bright work was nickel (enclosed bodies had oxidized silver hardware). Touring cars carried the new nonfolding trunk rack, and cloth upholstering was now available for them. Factory specifications and models for the third series are shown in the illustration.

A pressurized system of gasoline feed, which made gasoline flow more reliable than gravity feed, was new this year. This change was necessary because of a modification in the frame that lowered the center of the frame, the body and the running boards by three inches. With the rear-mounted gasoline tank pressurized, the position of the carburetor could be elevated for easier accessibility. The starter was changed to a dash-mounted pushbutton, and a Yale ignition lock was attached for security.

Pierce-Arrow's so-called production cars were actually custom-made. This made them costly to build and even more costly to purchase. Although it helped establish their luxury image, it also led to a financial crisis later.

Changes in the Wind

Although automobile sales were good during the early war years, the emphasis was shifting from automobile production to making trucks for military use. Truck sales were very good. Other auto manufacturers were unable to compete with Pierce in making as luxurious a car at a price that would leave a profit. Indeed, it was becoming increasingly difficult for Pierce to do so, with so many custom variations available. With many car makers competing in the market, innovations were produced rapidly to catch the eye of the potential buyer. At a time when the Pierce-Arrow management needed to change its thinking, it was stifled by the conservatism of the "old guard" (Fergusson, May and Sheppy).

In September 1914, Cadillac brought out its new V-8 engine. Packard introduced its big "twin six" in 1915. The Pierce-Arrow engineering department under Dave Fergusson was also working on a new V-8 (bore 3½ inch, storke 5¼ inch) in 1914. The actual displacement, however, was not much different from that of the 38-horsepower engine (4 inch x 5½ inch).

The conservative Pierce-Arrow board of directors chose to stay with the tried and true six-cylinder engine that had been a successful workhorse for the previous seven years. The board's failure to recognize public demand for, and the industry's trend towards, multicylinder engines was probably one of the company's earliest mistakes. This decision was the harbinger of a decline in sales and profits in years to come.

Actually Pierce had two of its biggest years during 1915 and 1916. Profits were in excess of $4 million both years. In 1917–18 profits decreased despite an increase in orders, partly due to an extensive building program. Truck production and sales did grow quite rapidly, and the two-ton and five-ton trucks were not cheap compared to those of other manufacturers. Testimonials from France during the war attested to the high quality and reliability of Pierce trucks.

Our War Department ordered 1,500 one-and-a-half ton trucks, and in August of 1918 placed a $20 million order for airplane engines of the Hispano-Suiza design. Unfortunately, six months later the Armistice meant cancellation of the order. One-third of the U.S. Government's truck order (500 units) was also cancelled.

With orders piling up, in 1916 the company was in a good financial position for expansion. That year the plant was enlarged to forty-five acres. Although the cost was written off as an expense, the construction cut into profits. Unfortunately, within two years orders fell off drastically.

By the end of 1916 Pierce-Arrow had decided that the company was too large for private ownership and went public. The New York City banking firm of J. and W. Seligman and Company handled the sale of 100,000 shares of preferred stock and 250,000 shares of common stock, for $10.7 million. Late in 1916, George Birge retired as president after seven years. He sold 7,000 shares of his 15,000 shares of Pierce-Arrow stock for $7 million in cash. Colonel Clifton became president, serving until 1918, with Henry May as vice president and Walter C. Wrye as treasurer. In 1918 Clifton moved over to become chairman of the board, and the presidency was filled by John C. Jay, Jr., a partner in the firm of J. and W. Seligman. The years after the war produced rapid change in management, philosophy and image. As Colonel Clifton had predicted in 1914, "things would never be the same."

Presidential Pierce-Arrows

In 1909 the White House switched from horse-drawn carriages to motorized vehicles for presidential use. Taft was the first President to use a fleet of cars in the White House. The two Pierce-Arrows purchased in 1909 were replaced periodically with new Pierce-Arrows.

During President Wilson's term in office, the White House garage held four Pierce-Arrows. Older models were replaced in 1916 with a 66-A-4 Vestibule Suburban, which was President Wilson's touring car. After his term of office ended March 4, 1921, he purchased the White House 1919 Pierce-Arrow 48-horsepower Vestibule Suburban (number 511121). He used it until his death in 1924. This restored car now resides at the Woodrow Wilson Birthplace Foundation, Staunton, Virginia.

For many years the government had the good taste to use Pierce-Arrows. During President Coolidge's term the White House had five automobiles, all Pierce-Arrows. These were leased from the company and replaced as necessary.

Series Four (1916–18)

The fourth series, from December 1915 until August 1918, produced the same designs and same three chassis, although a new French Brougham, convertible Roadster, and four-passenger Roadster were added. The new Town Brougham was brought out mid-series in 1917 at $5,900. Recension data published by the Pierce-Arrow Company in 1919 showed separate first, second, and third production runs during the three years. The three chassis types were manufactured sequentially and not concomitantly. The 48-B-4 chassis was most popular, and the emphasis was on production of this model. Only about 500 of the gigantic 66-A-4 cars were produced in the two and one-half years and less than ten survive. Their gasoline consumption was voracious at four miles to the gallon, especially during the war shortages, and the 48-B-4 performed nearly as well as the larger car anyway. Also, good cord tires lasted only about 6,000 miles on the heavy cars. By the end of 1918 production of the 38-horsepower and 66-horsepower models was discontinued, bringing to an end six years of manufacture. Because war effort production concentrated on trucks, only 100 48-horsepower models were made between June 1918 and May 1919. These cars used the new

Available Series-Four Models and Prices

	38-C-4		48-B-4		66-A-4	
	First Run	Second Run	First Run	Second Run	First Run	Second Run
2- or 3-Passenger Runabout	$4,300	$4,800	$4,900	$5,400	$5,900	$6,400
2- or 3-Passenger Coupe	$5,000	$5,700	$5,700	$6,400	$6,700	$7,400
4- or 5-Passenger Touring	$4,300	$4,800	$4,900	$5,400	$5,900	$6,400
7-Passenger Touring	—	—	$5,000	$5,500	$6,000	$6,500
Brougham	$5,200	$5,900	$5,800	$6,600	$6,800	$7,600
Landaulet	$5,200	$5,900	—	—	—	—
Sedan	$5,200	$5,900	—	—	—	—
Vestibule Landaulet	$5,350	$6,100	—	—	—	—
Vestibule Brougham Landaulet	$5,350	$6,100	—	—	—	—
Brougham Landaulet	$5,200	$5,900	—	—	—	—
Vestibule Brougham	$5,350	$6,100	$5,950	$6,800	$6,950	$7,800
Suburban	—	—	$6,000	$6,800	$7,000	$7,800
Landau	—	—	$6,000	$6,800	$7,000	$7,800
Suburban Landau	—	—	$6,000	$6,800	$7,000	$7,800
Vestibule Suburban	—	—	$6,200	$7,000	—	—
Vestibule Suburban Landau	—	—	$6,200	$7,000	$7,200	$8,000
Vestibule Landau	—	—	$6,200	$7,000	$7,200	$8,000
1917 SECOND-RUN MODELS:						
French Brougham	—	$5,900	—	—	—	—
French Brougham Landaulet	—	$5,900	—	—	—	—
Town Brougham	—	$5,900	—	—	—	—
2- or 3-Passenger Convertible Roadster	—	$5,700	—	$6,400	—	$7,400
4-Passenger Roadster	—	$4,800	—	—	—	—

dual-valve engine and were called the Series Five cars. In the eleven years after the 65-horsepower big six was introduced in 1907, about 1,600 of the huge chassis were made. The Pierce-Arrow Roster lists about fifteen remaining. Factory pictures show a 66-A-5 engine of dual-valve design. A 66-horsepower dual-valve engine was designed experimentally, but was never available as a standard model; only the 48-horsepower dual-valve engine was available. A very few dual-valve 66-horsepower engines were actually placed in cars and sold; one is presently in the Harrah Automobile Collection. Total production of the fourth series was about 4,900 cars. Prices ranged from $4,300 for the two-passenger Runabout to $7,200 for the Vestibule Suburban-Landau. Increased production costs made a $500 rise in price necessary in December 1916. Two new features in the Series Four cars were

the Westinghouse ignition system that replaced the commutator, and a coil thermostat to regulate the engine temperature.

The passing of the big "66" signified the end of an era. The war had changed many attitudes, and there was no longer much demand for that type of automobile. Peerless, which had a similar large model, dropped it in 1914.

Pierce tended to hang onto the same styles through changing tastes, which brought falling sales and financial trouble. Still, the Pierce-Arrows of those years were magnificent machines; they represented the company's "finest hour."

Series Five (1918–19)

When the company elected to stay with the six-cylinder engine, instead of the eight or twelve cylinders that competitors were using, Pierce had to make some changes to stay competitive in power. In July 1918, the company announced the arrival of its new 48-B-5 series with its dual-valve engine, and it projected 1,000 units would be available during the following year. Of those about ten survive.

The dual-valve engine was still a "T" design cast in pairs. It had two intake valves on one side and two exhaust valves on the other side of the block. The head was detachable. Having dual intake and exhaust valves for each cylinder allowed more flow area without making the size of a single valve unwieldly. Performance was comparable to that of the eight- and twelve-cylinder engines, but it did not have the same appeal to the postwar motoring market. Fergusson extolled the virtues of the new dual-valve engine (perhaps he was paranoid about his mere six cylinders), and indeed it did run well. Duesenberg also came out with a dual-valve racing engine in 1916. Horsepower was increased by 40 per cent. Acceleration was increased 20 per cent; gas consumption was improved by 11 per cent. The maximum speed was 72 mph at 2,500 rpm. The dual-valve principle, with modifications in the block, was used through 1928 (Model 36) before it was discontinued in favor of a straight eight. Pierce may not have been progressive, but it maintained quality workmanship.

The engine was six cylinders, cast in pairs with detachable heads. Later, dual-valve engines would be cast "en bloc." Bore and stroke were 4½ inches x 5½ inches with a horsepower rating of 48. The gas tank held 32 gallons, and total weight was 2½ tons. All models had 142-inch wheelbases, and body styles were similar to those of the Series Four. The four-passenger Roadster and French Brougham, new in the fourth series, appeared again in the fifth series and added to the surfeit of variations available.

Since virtually any combination could be obtained, these were still, in effect, custom automobiles. However, the time, labor and cost of producing these cars were making Pierce inefficient and noncompetitive. As in 1909, there were too many different models.

Available Series-Five Models (1918– 1919)

Body Type	Price
Two- and Three-Passenger Runabouts	$6,400
Two- and Three-Passenger Coupe	$7,500
Two- and Three-Passenger Convertible Roadster	$7,500
Four-Passenger Roadster	$6,400
Four-Passenger Touring	$6,400
Five-Passenger Touring	$6,400
Seven-Passenger Touring	$6,500
Brougham, Dome or Flat Roof	$7,800
Brougham Landaulet	$7,800
French Brougham	$7,800
French Brougham Landaulet	$7,800
Suburban, Dome or Flat Roof	$8,000
Landau, Dome	$8,000
Suburban Landau, Flat	$8,000
Vestibule Brougham, Dome or Flat	$8,000
Vestibule Brougham Landau, Flat	$8,000
Vestibule Suburban, Dome or Flat	$8,200
Vestibule Landau, Dome Roof	$8,200
Vestibule Suburban Landau, Flat	$8,200

The price of all models increased about $1,000 once civilian production was resumed. The prices were high—too high—and everyone knew it. Packard and Cadillac, which were becoming formidable competitors in the luxury field, were available at prices from $2,000 to $3,000 less than Pierce. In the late 1920s Packard and Cadillac styling would leave Pierce in the dust.

The "war to end all wars" was over. The world had changed, and so had Pierce-Arrow, and more change was coming. Pierce was no longer a management-owned firm. Their cars were magnificent, but they were becoming old-fashioned. Prices were too high and competition too stiff. The company whose philosophy once had been "The cost be damned," now had to answer to its stockholders. The good old days were gone.

. . . making its appearance in 1914 was the Westinghouse electric starter (replacing the old compressed-air starter) and generator. The starter was activated by a floor pedal. Along with the electric lights of Series One, the cars now had a complete electrical system.

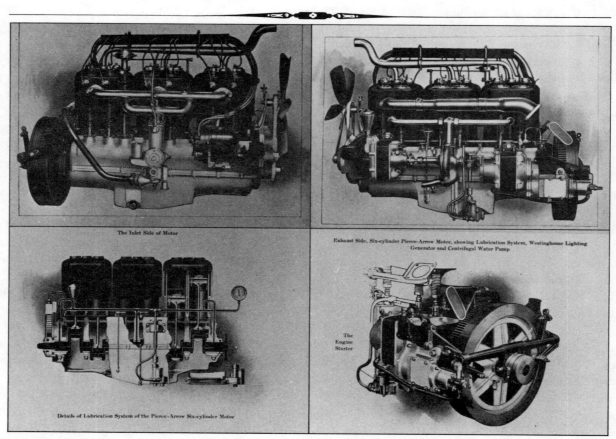

The Inlet Side of Motor

Exhaust Side, Six-cylinder Pierce-Arrow Motor, showing Lubrication System, Westinghouse Lighting Generator and Centrifugal Water Pump

Details of Lubrication System of the Pierce-Arrow Six-cylinder Motor

The Engine Starter

Details of the Series 2 engine (1914). This was the first model to have the electrical starter and generator. (Courtesy of the Motor Vehicle Manufacturers Association.)

66 Horse-power, Six-cylinder Pierce-Arrow Touring Car, Model A2, seating five persons

66 Horse-power, Six-cylinder Pierce-Arrow Landau, Model A4, seating seven persons

66 Horse-power, Six-cylinder Pierce-Arrow Vestibule Suburban, Model A2, seating seven persons

66 Horse-power, Six-cylinder Pierce-Arrow Touring Car, Model A2, seating seven persons

Top—A Series 2 Runabout. This was the first year and model of the fender-mounted headlights. The convex curve was later changed to concave (until 1933). (Courtesy of the Motor Vehicle Manufacturers Association.) *Center and bottom*—Series 2 models, made from May 1913 to July 1914. The electric side lights were integral with the cowl. (Courtesy of the University of Michigan.)

A Series 3 Victoria Runabout and a 66-A-3 Touring. The spring-loaded front bumper was standard from this series on (1915). The headlight curvature was changed to concave. (Courtesy of the University of Michigan.)

A 1915, 38-C-3 Touring. Note the trunk rack. (Courtesy of the University of Michigan.)

Top and center—Series 3 (1915) two- and three-passenger Runabouts. The tires were mounted on Johnson demountable rims. (Courtesy of the University of Michigan.) *Bottom*—A Series 3 Touring with an unusual (California-type) top. (Courtesy of the University of Michigan.)

Top—An open Brougham Landaulet. (Courtesy of the University of Michigan.) *Center and bottom*—A Series 3 five-passenger Sedan and a Brougham. (Courtesy of the University of Michigan.)

A 1915, 38-C-3 Brougham and Vestibule Brougham Landaulet—stately carriages! The chauffeur's quarters were enclosed in the vestibule models. (Courtesy of the University of Michigan.)

SPECIFICATIONS OF PIERCE-ARROW MOTOR CARS
ALL MODELS WILL HAVE:

No. of Cylinders	Six, cast in pairs.
Ignition	Two complete and separate systems: first, jump spark, 6 individual units, with one master vibrator; second, Bosch high-tension magneto.
Battery Equipment	One set storage.
Carburetor	Pierce-Arrow automatic.
Control	Hand throttle and foot accelerator.
Oiling	Pressure feed to all crank-shaft and pin bearings, cylinders and pistons.
Transmission	Selective, sliding gears, direct on high speed; side lever control, bevel gear drive.
Speeds	Four forward and reverse.
Bearings	Ball and roller bearings all over except motor.
Springs	Front, semi-elliptic; rear, three-quarter elliptic.
Regular Tires	Goodrich, "Silvertown", front and rear.
Brakes	Equalized foot brakes on inside of drums on hubs, both rear wheels. Equalized hand brakes on outside of drums on hubs, both rear wheels.
Rims	Pierce-Arrow demountable (Johnson patent) with quick detachable channels.
Clutch	Cone, leather faced, running in oil.
Front Axle	Drop-forged, I-beam, special steel, heat treated.
Rear Axle	Semi-floating.
Steering Gear	Screws and nut.

	Model 38 C-3	Model 48 B-3	Model 66 A-3
Cylinder Dimensions	4 x 5½ in.	4½ x 5½ in.	5 x 7 in.
Revolutions per Minute	200 to 2000.	150 to 1800.	150 to 1600.
Gasoline Capacity	All models, 26 gals.	All models, 32 gals.	All models, 32 gals.
Wheel Base	All models, 134 ins.	All models, 142 ins.	All models, 147½ in.
Tread	56 in.	56 in.	57 in.
Wheels	Wood, artillery; all models, 36 in. all around.	Wood, artillery; all models, 37 in. all around.	Wood, artillery; runabout, 37 in. all around; other models, 37 in. front, 38 in. rear.
Tire Dimensions	All models, 4½ in.	All models, 5 ins.	Runabout, 5 in. all around; other models, 5 in. front, 5½ in. rear.

PRICES F. O. B. BUFFALO

Model 38 C-3		Model 48 B-3		Model 66 A-3	
Runabout	$4300	Runabout	$4900	Runabout	$5900
Coupé Runabout	4575	Coupé Runabout	5175	Coupé Runabout	6175
Touring, 4-Passenger	4300	Touring, 4-Passenger	4900	Touring, 4-Passenger	5900
Touring, 5-Passenger	4300	Touring, 5-Passenger	4900	Touring, 5-Passenger	5900
Brougham	5200	Touring, 7-Passenger	5000	Touring, 7-Passenger	6000
Landaulet	5200	Brougham	5800	Brougham	6800
Vestibule Broughamn	5350	Suburban	6000	Suburban	7000
Vestibule Landaulet	5350	Landau	6000	Landau	7000
Brougham-Landaulet	5200	Suburban-Landau	6000	Suburban-Landau	7000
Vestibule Brougham-Landaulet	5350	Vestibule Suburban	6200	Vestibule Suburban	7200
		Vestibule Landau	6200	Vestibule Landau	7200
		Vestibule Brougham	5950	Vestibule Brougham	6950
		Vestibule Suburban-Landau	6200	Vestibule Suburban-Landau	7200

REGULAR EQUIPMENT FOR ALL PIERCE-ARROW MODELS

Electric generator, special storage battery and starter.
Two electric head lamps
Two electric side lamps
One electric rear lamp and number illuminator.
One dash instrument lamp.
Two tonneau lamps in touring car.
One extension lamp.

Pierce-Arrow power-driven air pump for inflating tires.
Bulb horn.
Klaxon electric horn.
Full set of tools.
Warner speedometer, autometer and clock.
Collision bumpers, front and rear.
Extra tire carriers with well in running board.

Coat and blanket rail.
Pierce-Arrow detachable trunk rack.
Folding foot rest, touring and enclosed.
Pierce-Arrow gasoline primer.
Gasoline gauge.
Yale locks, with universal key on hood, dash cabinets, tool compartments, tire carrier and ignition switch.

Series 3 specifications. (Courtesy of the University of Michigan.)

Top—A typical Pierce-Arrow army truck, circa 1917. The U.S. government ordered 1½-ton trucks (at $3,500 each). England and France ordered 2- and 5-ton trucks. (Courtesy of the University of Michigan.)
Bottom—Pierce-Arrow army trucks ready for shipment overseas. (Where are they now?)
(Courtesy of the Pierce-Arrow Society.)

Top—The Pierce-Arrow plant expanded in 1916 to 45 acres (a 1930 photograph).
(Courtesy of the University of Michigan.) *Center and bottom*—Two styles of Series 4 Vestibule Suburbans,
66-A-4 and 38-C-4. Note the United States seal on the upper car denoting President Wilson's White House car.
(Courtesy of the University of Michigan.)

$10,000,000.

THE PIERCE-ARROW MOTOR CAR CO.

EIGHT PER CENT. CUMULATIVE CONVERTIBLE PREFERRED STOCK.

*Convertible share for share into common shares
at option of holder.*

Central Trust Company of New York,   The Chase National Bank of the City of New York
Transfer Agent   Registrar

Incorporated under the laws of the State of New York.

Preferred as to assets as well as dividends. Redeemable in whole or in part, at option of the Company, on any dividend date, on sixty days' notice, at 125 and accrued dividends. Quarterly Dividends payable on the first days of January, April, July and October.

CAPITALIZATION.

Authorized and outstanding
Preferred Stock, 100,000 shares—par value $100—$10,000,000.
Common Stock, 250,000 shares—without par value.
NO MORTGAGE OR OTHER BONDED INDEBTEDNESS OUTSTANDING

The Company must devote to the purchase of preferred stock in the market or by call at 125 and accrued dividends an amount of cash equal to whatever amount is paid in any year in cash dividends on the common stock over and above $5.00 per share. The preferred stock so retired, and preferred stock otherwise redeemed by the Company, will be converted into common stock and held in the treasury to be used for the general purposes of the Company, or for distribution as a stock dividend on outstanding common shares.

Stockholders have no rights of subscription to stock or securities convertible into stock if issued for property, and preferred stockholders have no rights of subscription except to preferred stock or securities convertible into preferred stock.

Reference is made to the annexed letter dated December 7, 1916 of Charles Clifton, Esq., President of The Pierce-Arrow Motor Car Co., to the report to us of Messrs. Price, Waterhouse & Co. dated December 1, 1916 and to the accounts for the year ending December 31, 1916, certified by Price, Waterhouse & Co. from which we summarize as follows:

1.—The Company manufactures the well-known Pierce-Arrow pleasure car and Pierce-Arrow truck. It owns a thoroughly modern, well-equipped plant at Buffalo.

2.—Physical Assets at December 31, 1916, after setting apart cash to retire the bonds of the old Company, amounted to $15,573,000., whereof $11,090,000. net working assets.

3.—Earnings since July 1, 1911, from one and one-half to five times the preferred dividend; for year ending December 31, 1916 equal to over five times the preferred dividend.

4.—Attention is called to the provision whereby there will be devoted to the retirement of preferred stock an amount of cash equal to any amount paid in cash dividends on common stock above $5.00 per share per annum.

All legal details incident to incorporation have been under the supervision of Messrs. Cravath & Henderson, of New York City.

APPLICATION WILL BE MADE TO LIST THESE SHARES ON
THE NEW YORK STOCK EXCHANGE

We recommend the above described Preferred Stock of The Pierce-Arrow Motor Car Co. for investment.

J. & W. SELIGMAN & CO.
NEW YORK

March 1, 1917

The above information has been obtained from sources we believe to be reliable,
but is not guaranteed.

A March 1917 stock-offering prospectus from the J. and W. Seligman Company.
(Courtesy of Bernie Weis.)

A 48-B-4 Victoria Runabout and 66-A-4 Touring. The photograph belies the fact that these were huge automobiles. (Courtesy of the University of Michigan.)

A 1916, 66-A-4, four-passenger Roadster, new with this series. The same model was used by the Akron, Ohio, fire department with a rear-mounted tank. (Courtesy of the University of Michigan.)

For many years the government had the good taste to use Pierce-Arrows. During President Coolidge's term the White House had five automobiles, all Pierce-Arrows. These were leased from the company and replaced as necessary.

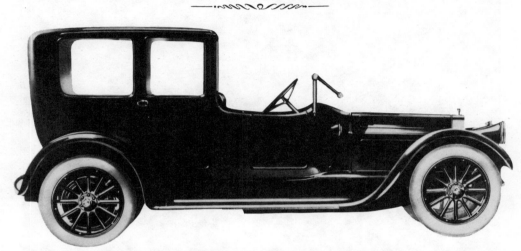

A 38-C-4 Town Brougham, new during mid-Series 4, and a 66-A-4 three-passenger coupe.

Top and center—A 1917 (38-C-4) Landaulet, open and closed. The Series 4 cars were produced between December 1914 and August 1918 in 3 "runs." (Courtesy of the University of Michigan.)
Bottom—A few cars along "Great Arrow Avenue" at the factory. The 38-C-4 Brougham shows the detachable top over the chauffeur's compartment. (Courtesy of the University of Michigan.)

Top—A Series 4 dashboard. In the cluster of instruments are a clock, odometer, speedometer, oil pressure, ammeter, gasoline tank pressure gauge, light switches, and Westinghouse ignition switch. (Courtesy of the University of Michigan.) *Bottom*—A Series 4 engine. (Courtesy of the Motor Vehicle Manufacturers Association.)

Top—A special-order Series 4 Touring with wire wheels and dual windshield.
(Courtesy of the University of Michigan.) *Bottom*—Going calling, 1917 style, in a Series 4 Brougham.
(Courtesy of the University of Michigan.)

Top—A built-in luggage case on the running board, circa 1917. (Courtesy of the University of Michigan.)
Center—The Pierce-Arrow factory, 1917. (Courtesy of the Pierce-Arrow Society.) *Bottom*—The World War I
memorial plaque designed by Herbert Dawley and erected on the Pierce-Arrow building May 30, 1919.
Thirty-two employees died of the 2,200 who served. (Courtesy of the Pierce-Arrow Society.)

The photos here were released by the factory and demonstrate that the Touring top can be put up by one man (if he's half monkey and half contortionist), circa 1917. (Courtesy of the University of Michigan.)

Examples of custom monograms on Series 4 automobiles. (Courtesy of the Pierce-Arrow Society.)

The only engine that was standard in the Series 5 cars was the 48-horsepower dual-valve engine. Yet this factory drawing shows a 66-A-5 dual-valve engine. It apparently was never made in any quantity, yet a few were actually sold in cars. One survives in the Harrah's automobile collection. (Courtesy of the University of Michigan.)

The Series 5 models were quite similar externally to those of Series 4. These were built from June 1918 until May 1919. (Courtesy of the Motor Vehicle Manufacturers Association.)

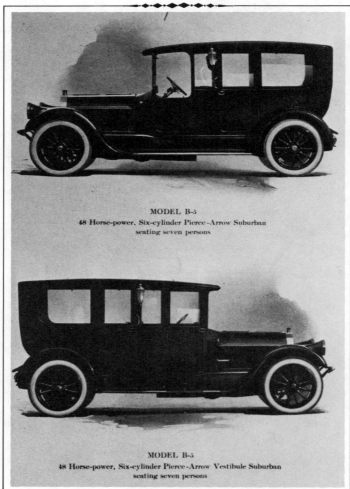

MODEL B-5
48 Horse-power, Six-cylinder Pierce-Arrow Suburban
seating seven persons

MODEL B-5
48 Horse-power, Six-cylinder Pierce-Arrow Vestibule Suburban
seating seven persons

The enclosed models of Series 5. (Courtesy of the Motor Vehicle Manufacturers Association.)

6
POST WAR CHANGE
1919–28

The big shakeup in management, the "debacle," as Herbert Dawley later called it, actually began in 1916 and went on for the next seven years. The first step was the change from private to public ownership in 1916, with the sale of 350,000 shares of stock. Birge retired in late 1916 and Colonel Clifton became the new president. At this time, Henry May, unable to watch the old employees go, also retired. He had been vice president at Pierce since 1896. Clifton advised Herbert Dawley that changes were coming, and that Dawley ought to look after his own future. Dawley left Pierce-Arrow in 1917 for a good job offer. Lawrence H. Gardner, the longtime secretary, retired, and his brother, William H. Gardner, was dead. Fergusson as chief engineer, Charles Sheppy and James Way continued with Pierce, and in a large measure were responsible for the lack of progressive thinking in the company after the war.

Profits peaked at $4.3 million in 1915 and then declined steadily to half of that by 1918. It was in 1918 that Colonel Clifton became chairman of the board and John C. Jay, Jr. the new president. Jay had been a partner in the Seligman banking firm and also a partner in the George W. Goethals engineering firm, of Panama Canal fame. With him came Colonel George W. Mixter as vice president and general manager of Pierce-Arrow. Mixter had also been a partner in the Goethals firm. Not surprisingly, the following year, the George M. Goethals Company was retained to provide engineering guidance for the Pierce-Arrow Company. During its brief association with Pierce-Arrow, changes in personnel were frequent. The housecleaning was the most drastic in the forty years of the company's history. The personnel from Seligman and Goethals who were brought into Pierce-Arrow were intelligent businessmen but were not experienced in the manufacturing of automobiles. They were paid to solve the financial problems of Pierce-Arrow, but they didn't have "cars in their blood." A major change in management had occurred, and a similar redesigning of the Pierce-Arrow car and trucks was deemed necessary, and correctly so, in the new postwar era. The dual valve engine was new in 1918, but it was not the progressive step that the company needed. The Series Five cars of 1918–19 were quite similar in all respects, except the engine, to the previous four series. The cars of the past several years were magnificent, but a new look was needed.

Series 31 and 51 (1919–20)
In 1919 two new models were introduced: the Series 31 and 51. These were produced in 1919 and 1920. The models were so designated because the serial numbers and engine numbers began with those two numbers, 311,001 through 312,375 in 1919; 313,001 through 314,500 in 1920 and 511,001 through

513,300 in 1919; 514,001 through 515,700 in 1920. Despite the large range of serial numbers, only 4,000 units were shipped (many groups of numbers were skipped).

The "31" had a 38-horsepower dual-valve engine (4 inch x 5½ inch) on a 134-inch wheelbase, while the "51" had a 48-horsepower dual-valve engine (4½ inch x 5½ inch) on a 142-inch wheelbase. The new Delco dual distributor was two tandem units. The cars were still sizable at 5,100 pounds, although shorter than the previous 147½-inch chassis. Body styles were again similar to the Runabouts, Touring, various Suburbans and Landaus. The two ventilators on the top of the hood were no longer used. The instrument panels were redesigned as one piece integral with the body. A Klaxon horn was retained, but the bulb horn on the steering column was no longer used. It was nostalgic, but just not effective for motoring in 1920. The radiator core was changed to one of hexagonal tubes. The headlights contained a second bulb, which replaced the cowl side lamps. There were still too many variations, about twenty-five. Prices ranged from $7,250 to $9,250 (Cadillacs were about $4,000 to $5,000). Profits in 1920 slipped again, to a new low of $2 million.

In 1920, John Jay, after two years as president, was replaced by Colonel George W. Mixter. However, Jay stayed with Pierce on the board of directors until 1934. Succeeding Mixter as vice president and general manager was George M. Graham. Mixter had been a partner with the Seligman banking firm, and a colonel during the war in airplane production. He remained as Pierce-Arrow president from 1920 until he resigned at the end of 1921. After Mixter's resignation, Colonel Clifton ran the company until Myron Forbes assumed the presidency. In the summer of 1921 the Goethals firm ceased its association with Pierce-Arrow, after two years of reorganization.

Very shortly after assuming the presidency in 1920, Mixter announced to the dealers his plans for sweeping changes in the types of automobiles manufactured by the company. First, there was to be only one chassis produced, known as the Pierce-Arrow (or Series 32). The engineering design would maximize performance. Completely new styles would be lower and smoother in appearance. Only ten styles would be made, compared to sixty in the past decade. Another major innovation was to change the traditional cast

aluminum bodies to 14-gauge ($^3/_{32}$-inch) sheet aluminum over wooden ash frames. Cast aluminum was still used, however, in certain key places, such as around the window moldings. The resulting cars were lighter in weight. Mixter was the prime mover in this rather radical design change. The Leon Rubay body-building company of Cleveland (with the help of James Way and Fergusson of Pierce-Arrow) was hired for the actual body design. A few years later the Rubay Company went out of business. The cost of the conversion, additional machinery and tooling was nearly $2 million. Unfortunately, this was not a propitious time for such a sizable expenditure by the company. The depression of 1921 was a short but rather severe one, especially for builders of expensive automobiles. That year Pierce lost $8 million. Orders for cars with variations from the standard bodies were discouraged by the company to minimize production costs. By April 1920, testing was already begun on what was to be the new Series 32 of 1921. Unfortunately, problems with the car caused many to be returned for repairs. The carburetors did not work well, and the engines needed to be reworked. Sheppy, who had left Pierce, was rehired to help troubleshoot the Series 32.

The year 1921 also saw Dave Fergusson quit as chief engineer after twenty years with the company. He had been frustrated by the recent changes at Pierce. He went on to the Cunningham Company in Rochester, New York, retired in 1950, and died a year later at the age of eighty-one. Fergusson was replaced briefly by Delmar G. "Barney" Roos, a name well known in automotive history.

Roos was born in 1888 in New York City and was educated at Cornell University. After working for seven years at Locomobile, he joined Pierce-Arrow in 1919 as assistant to the chief engineer. He became acting chief engineer in 1921 but, unhappy with the Pierce management and policies, he left later that same year. He returned to Locomobile as vice president of engineering, then went to Marmon in 1925. Ironically, a decade later he was working for Studebaker when they merged with Pierce-Arrow. He died in 1960, after introducing numerous "firsts" during his long career: mechanical fuel pump; ball-bearing spring shackles; free wheeling; and carburetor silencer. He was also instrumental in the development of the Jeep. Charles Sheppy, a Pierce engineer from the Motorette days, then moved into the position of chief engineer in 1921 and held that position until his death in 1927.

Colonel Clifton, the Grand Old Man of Pierce-Arrow, retired from the board in 1921. He remained active in automobile circles (president of the National Automobile Chamber of Commerce, 1913 to 1927), until his death in 1928 at seventy-four. In his twenty-five years with Pierce, he had a tremendous influence on the character and philosophy of the company. He also exerted considerable influence over the whole industry.

By 1921 practically none of the Old Guard was left at Pierce. Postwar change made it a different company, with different management and philosophy. The personal character and ideals of the founders were no longer present at Pierce-Arrow.

Series 32 (1920–21)

The Series 32 was the all-new Pierce-Arrow that President Mixter had been instrumental in bringing about. This was the car that was supposed to make Pierce more competitive and revitalize sales. Its hurried development and testing occurred in the spring of 1920. A touring model test car was driven by Davis, Talcott and Hodge to the West Coast and back, to prove the car's reliability. It performed quite well under unfavorable road conditions. The Series 32 was available later in 1920 through 1921. Compared to the classic lines of the early 1930s, the Series 32 was boxy. But compared to the "monster cars" (as Fergusson referred to the Pierces of the teens), these new styles were quite a radical change from the Pierces of the past. The company was quite proud of the new look. Despite some mechanical problems and a design that was in some ways antiquated, it was a good car with traditional Pierce high-quality workmanship.

Only one chassis was available. This had a 138-inch wheelbase with dual-valve, 38-horsepower engine. Although still the old-fashioned "T" head, six-cylinder design, the new engine was now cast "en bloc," instead of in pairs, with a removable head. The "en bloc" design caused less vibration. Most of the industry had by this time gone to the "L" head engine, and engines of at least eight cylinders were the rule of the big cars. Pierce, like Rolls-Royce, held on to its six and defended the car's design with quality workmanship and performance.

The bore and stroke were 4 inches x 5½ inches. By

increasing the maximum engine rpm to 3,000 and changing the rear-end ratio to 4.285 to 1, the designers were able to get pretty decent performance out of the 38-horsepower engine. Acceleration was improved and gasoline consumption was about 12 miles per gallon. Weight was about 4,700 pounds, and the price was in the $6,500 to $8,500 range.

The new engine also had a new Delco dual-ignition system with two separate distributors and two spark plugs for each cylinder. The two banks of spark plugs could be operated separately or in unison, by control switches on the dashboard. The old cone clutch, used for twenty years, was discarded for the new multiple-disc dry plate clutch with asbestos facings. The Alemite greasing system was also new, as was the Stromberg-made carburetor. The dash was integrated with the body, and the cluster of instruments illuminated under a glass cover. A gasoline priming pump and an air-pressure gauge were added to the dash, and a fuel gauge was placed on the rear-mounted 26-gallon tank. The transmission was changed to three forward sliding gears; with the redesign of the engine and rear-end ratios, four forward gears were no longer necessary. The top speed was a respectable 72 miles per hour. A weak point in this dual-valve engine was its thin walls between the cylinders and valves, with a tendency toward cracking the block that made it imperative to run the engine "cool" (i.e., not too lean).

At long last, the steering wheel was moved to the left side and the gearshift and parking brake were located centrally (changes long resisted by Fergusson). In the summer of 1911, the Mays and Fergussons toured in a 48-horsepower Pierce-Arrow that had an experimental left-hand drive, but Fergusson's impressions after driving it were not favorable. Most auto manufacturers had long since changed over from right-hand drive; this changeover started about 1912.

The enclosed cars had fixed sun visors, and some models had split windshields for ventilation. Although factory pictures of the models generally showed drum headlights, most cars sold had fender headlights. Apparently most custom body designers did not want to be limited to fender headlights.

Unfortunately, the new design and improved performance was not enough to offset the recession of 1921. Sales were down 50 percent and the company lost $8 million. The number of employees dropped to 1,800 men from about 9,500 during the war. Needless to say, the modern new facilities were working well below capacity. The need was increased sales volume.

Management by the Goethals Company ended in May 1921. In November 1922, President Mixter was replaced by Myron Edison Forbes. During his brief term as president, Mixter had done much to update the company's product, but the economic climate at that time had been a strong negative force. And the "new" Series 32 had its share of mechanical problems.

Myron Forbes (1880–1966) was born in Jarvisburg, North Carolina. After working in Norfolk, Virginia, for ten years with the accounting firm of Hoskins and Sells, he moved to Buffalo in 1919 as treasurer of the Pierce-Arrow Company. In 1921 he moved up to vice president, replacing George Graham.

Forbes was an energetic person who instilled a feeling of optimism into the company. He was the Alfred Sloan of Pierce-Arrow.

Since 1908 when Billy Durant had formed General Motors, taking Buick and merging other companies (Cadillac, Chevrolet, etc.) into the fold, rumors of merger were frequent in the auto industry. Right after the war there had been talk of a financial connection between Pierce-Arrow and General Motors. By 1921 Pierce-Arrow was in a difficult position financially, and in April 1922 plans were announced for a merger with Lafayette. The Lafayette automobile, owned by Nash, was manufactured just before the recession of 1921 and was hard hit by that recession. Lafayette made an expensive automobile and was beset with financial problems; a merger would bring security. Colonel Clifton was to be called back from retirement at sixty-eight to be president of the dual company, and Charles Nash was chosen as chairman of the board. Since business at Pierce suddenly began picking up in 1922, perhaps the directors felt that the merger was not necessary. At any rate, within a month the merger was called off. Two years later, Lafayette went out of business. Lafayette had needed Pierce-Arrow more than the reverse.

In 1925 rumors of merger again circulated, this time with American Car and Foundry. It also came to naught. In 1923, American automobile manufacturers numbered 108; four years later the number had dropped to forty-four. After twenty years of growth and experience in making automobiles, competition in the industry had become fierce. Many other automobile companies besides Pierce were having finan-

cial and sales problems. The 1930s were to see many companies struggle for survival and die, including Pierce-Arrow.

By 1922, the recession had blown over. Forbes was the new energetic and enthusiastic president and general manager. Sales and profits were taking an upward turn. Car sales improved from 1,400 in 1921 to 5,600 in 1925. Truck sales went from 700 to 1,800 in the same period. The meager company profit of $10,000 in 1922 soared to $1,600,000 in 1925. Yearly, Pierce-Arrow's position became stronger, and credit for this was given to Myron Forbes. By 1923 sales had doubled from 1922, and morale was riding high.

Series 33 (1921–25)

Production of the Series 32 had run about one year (1920–21). Available company records are vague about the actual number of cars fabricated during this period. Probably less than 1,000 cars were made, and of these three examples survive today, making this model quite rare. The new Series 33 appeared in late 1921 and was produced through 1925. This model was almost identical to its predecessor, Series 32. The body styles were the same, but some new variations were added: French limousine; enclosed-drive limousine; and seven-passenger sedan. This brought the total up to twelve models. A differentiating feature between the two series was that the enclosed cars of the 32 had ring door handles, whereas in the 33 these were changed to a bar-type handle. Both the 32 and 33 models had a unique arrangement of the hood-louvers with the five louvers grouped at the rear of the hood. The chassis were basically the same, although the engine was modified somewhat. The two separate distributors used on the dual-valve engine were replaced in the later Series 33 models with one large double distributor. In the last year of production of the Series 33, the Automobile Manufacturers Association lists as standard equipment an automatic windshield cleaner and a winter front cover for the radiator. During the five-year period a few more than 6,000 Series 33 automobiles were made, and fewer than fifty survive. This was, unfortunately, fewer than Forbes had hoped to build. Production of the "33" ceased in early 1926. Prices ranged from $6,500 to $8,500 in 1922. Although the Series 33 was a very good car from the standpoint of quality and performance, it was just too expensive for the market. In 1923 prices were reduced by over a thousand dollars to the $5,250 to $7,000 range, to become more competitive. This spurred on sales and profits.

It became obvious that the cost of manufacturing and the price to the consumer were vital factors for Pierce-Arrow, as they were for all the other manufacturers struggling for survival. The price seemed especially high considering that an antiquated six-cylinder "T" engine design was still used. Quality could not compensate for old-fashioned design, and the public's taste was capricious.

Series 80 (1925–27)

As early as mid-1923, Forbes decided to produce a small six-cylinder car to enable Pierce-Arrow to enter the medium-priced field. He reasoned that lower prices would sell more cars, better utilize the large facilities and increase profits. The all-new car would have the same traditional Pierce quality but with a price tag that was $2,000 to $3,000 less than the Series 33. The Series 80 was introduced in August 1924, and sales skyrocketed. This success was abetted by the fact that the Pierce-Arrow Finance Corporation had been formed in August 1923, to enable buyers to pay for their cars on installments. Also, the number of Pierce-Arrow dealerships had been expanded greatly. The sudden growth in sales of the Series 80 was short-lived, however, and within two years it was necessary to reduce prices again to stimulate sales. The enthusiasm and growth of 1923 did not endure. By 1927, despite sales of more than 6,000 cars, the company lost nearly $1 million. Again they found themselves in a financial crisis.

The all-new "light six" model 80 was the design responsibility of Chief Engineer Charles Sheppy, although his assistants, John Talcott and Charles Pleuthner, probably should be given credit for the bulk of it. The chassis had a new "L" head (finally!) six-cylinder engine with a unit transmission. The engine was cast "en bloc" but was not dual-valve. Bore and stroke were 3½ inches x 5 inches and developed 70 horsepower at 2,800 rpm. The wheelbase was only 130 inches and the balloon-tire size (on wooden wheels) was reduced to 32 inches x 5.77 inches. Weight was about 4,700 pounds. The maximum speed was only 65 miles per hour. Four-wheel brakes had come in at the end of the Series 33 run in 1924, and were used on this new Series 80. The author has a late

1925 Series 33 which has four-wheel brakes and the new triple taillight like that on the Series 80. The clutch was changed to a *single* dry plate type. New Houdaille shock absorbers were used on the Series 80 in 1925. In 1926 venting of blow-by crankcase vapors into the carburetor was introduced.

Unlike the Series 33 which had the slanting windshield, the Series 80 returned to the vertical windshield, with the protruding visor. The side of the hood had louvers evenly-spaced along the full length of it. The triple-lamp taillight was used on all of the Model 80 cars. Actually, the triple light, which would be used for many years, first replaced the old single-lens light on the last run of the Series 33 cars in 1925. This Series 80 car was completely different from the Series 33. The "80" was less complex, less expensive, and parts were not interchangable with the Series 33. Custom bodies by Brunn, LeBaron, and Judkins were available, however, in the Series 80.

The exact production number of Model 80 cars is not available, but estimates for the three years are: 1925: 4,250; 1926: 7,500; 1927: 4,500. Despite the manufacture of about 16,000 of these cars, profits sagged. Many Model 80s are still around, and they are not as appealing to collectors as the larger and older Pierce-Arrows, or the classics of the 1930s.

The twelve body styles of the Model 80 were similar to those of Series 33 and were again becoming old-fashioned. Two new models were the convertible coupe with rumble seat, and five-passenger sport sedan Landau. Pierce-Arrow was falling behind companies like Packard, Cadillac and Lincoln when it came to styling. Those companies were to make some of the most beautifully-designed bodies of the "classical" period. (The true "classic" cars are limited to certain makes between 1925 and 1948.) Initially the Series 80 body styles available were limited, but later about seventeen variations were made, including Runabouts, Coupes, Sedans, Phaetons, Landaus, and Limousines. Prices ranged from $2,495 to $4,045. Although the "80" was a pretty good car, it could not compete with the cheaper Packards or Cadillacs. Decreasing sales caused the production of the Model 80 to cease at the end of 1927.

The Aluminum Pierce-Arrows

The Pierce Company had always been a proponent of aluminum in their automobiles. Beginning with the

Great Arrow of 1904, the bodies were made of cast aluminum, as were other parts (engine pans). In 1920 the company switched from cast aluminum to sheet aluminum bodies in the Series 32.

In the early 1920s, Alcoa took over the American Body Company of Buffalo, New York. During this period Alcoa became interested in building an all-aluminum car to promote more use of aluminum in the auto industry. This interest apparently had been stimulated by the English designer L. S. Pomeroy, when he visited Alcoa in 1919. Accurate information about the aluminum cars is spotty, but sometime about 1923 work was begun on possibly seven experimental cars. Four of those were built at the American Body Company in Buffalo. The engine and chassis were designed by L. S. Pomeroy, and the bodies (sedan, touring and coupe) were designed by John S. Burdick. Approximately 85 percent of the car's metal content was aluminum. The engine blocks were aluminum with cast-iron sleeves. In these cars, weight was reduced by about 1,000 pounds. The four-cylinder engines (3¼ inches x 5 inches) put out 75 horsepower at 3,000 rpm. These were driven and tested and about 1928 were dismantled and inspected for wear.

In addition to the four Pomeroy cars, three more cars were built with the assistance of Pierce-Arrow, all sedans with bodies basically in the Series 80 style. The engines, however, were the Pomeroy four-cylinder aluminum type. The aluminum Pierce-Arrows were used in comparison testing with the standard Series 80 Pierce-Arrows. A report dated September 29, 1926, indicated that the automobiles made by the American Body Company performed noticeably better than the aluminum Pierce-Arrows (for shame). The outcome of the testing, when concluded in 1928, is unknown, and the final disposition of the seven cars is also unknown except for the American Body Company-built car number 232 now in the Ford Museum. Ironically, after this investigation into the use of more aluminum in automobile production, Pierce-Arrow in future years used less aluminum.

Series 36 (1926–28)
Automobile design was moving toward lighter, sleeker, less expensive cars in the 1920s. The Series 80 was President Forbes's effort in this direction. Despite Pierce-Arrow's initial financial success with this

model, the company just couldn't escape its "prestigious-car" heritage. In late 1926 it brought out just what the public didn't need—the Series 36. This model was a reworked and embellished, albeit cheaper, Series 33. The Series 36 was available in 1927 and 1928. Although no accurate production figures are known, probably no more than 1,500 were made in 1927 and 500 in 1928; about 30 have survived. Series 36 cars made in 1928 (rather than 1927) can be distinguished by the Pierce Crest found in the front of the radiator shell. This also was featured on the Series 81 of 1928.

The Series 36 came in seventeen styles: Coupe; Touring; Sedan; and Limousine, ranging in price from $5,875 to $8,000. This price was still way beyond the average pocketbook, although financing was available. This model can be distinguished from its predecessor (Series 33) by the new triple-lamp taillight, and the hood louvers arranged in six clusters of three louvers each. New six-ply balloon tires were used in place of the previous straight-sided tires. Also new (after February 1924 and on late Series 33 cars) was the four-wheel vacuum-boost brake system, which applied 280 pounds of pressure to the brakes. Pierce was not an early advocate of hydraulic brake systems, realizing that an accidental leak in the system would cause a dangerous loss of brakes. In guessing future automotive trends, Pierce guessed wrong. In 1936 Pierce went to Bendix vacuum-assisted brakes. Houdaille shock absorbers were standard equipment after May 1925. Features similar to the Series 33 were the 138-inch wheelbase, 38.4-horsepower (NACC rating), 4-inch x 5½-inch dual-valve six-cylinder "T" engine, automatic windshield cleaners, three forward gears, dry multiple-disc clutch and power tire pump. Still striving to maintain the image of opulence, the company produced beautiful wood interiors, silk blinds, Wilton carpets, and gold-plated inside hardware. Designs were less than inspiring, but craftsmanship was still above reproach.

Series 81 (1928)
The shortcomings of the "light six" Model 80 were obvious, especially compared to the powerful engines evolving during this period—the Duesenberg, for example. Decreasing sales and profits made it necessary to look to improved performance of the Pierce-Arrow. As early as the fall of 1926, midway through

the Model 80 production span, Sheppy, Talcott, and Pleuthner were already redesigning the "80" engine. Having just been through the aluminum car experience with the Pomeroy engine, it was natural to consider utilizing more aluminum in the engine components. The connecting rods, pistons, and cylinder-head were changed to aluminum. The crankshaft strength was increased. With an increase of engine rpm from 2,800 to 3,200, the brake horsepower was boosted from 70 to 75 without changing the 3⅓ inch x 5 inch bore and stroke.

In late 1926 and early 1927, one hundred of these modified engines were installed in Series 80 chassis for field testing. Results were gratifying, and the last 500 cars of Series 80 run in 1927 contained the improved engine. These cars became the basis of the Series 81, which was announced November 10, 1927, and manufactured only through 1928.

Body styles of the Series 81 were like the Series 80 but more rounded. The 130-inch wheelbase remained the same. The roof was rounded and extended out over the windsl. ·ld as an integral visor. Front fenders extended more gracefully to the rear, and the fender headlamps were a smaller configuration, unique to this model. Apparently other people besides the author didn't like the headlight treatment of the Series 81, and in 1929 the headlight reverted once again to the typical Pierce-Arrow design. New with the Series 81 was the helmeted archer radiator cap, which was an option. As with fender headlights fourteen years earlier, this archer was synonymous with Pierce-Arrow and therefore prestigious to own. The archer was so consistently requested that it became in effect standard equipment. It wasn't until 1934 that the bare-headed archer was actually standard equipment, and then it could be omitted by special order.

Appearing on the radiator shell in the Series 81

(and the 1928 Series 36 as well), was the emblem said to be the crest of the Pierce family. According to Mrs. Percy Pierce, the crest is *not* that of the George N. Pierce family. Apparently the error was caught but not in time to be changed during 1928. By 1929 the crest had disappeared from the Pierce-Arrow radiators. In that one year nearly 5,000 Series 81 units were manufactured.

About twelve standard styles were available, and prices ranged from $2,900 for a Runabout to $3,550 for the seven-passenger enclosed-driver Limousine. These prices were only slightly higher for the corresponding Series 80 cars.

End of a Trying Decade

By 1928 the financial situation at Pierce-Arrow was again desperate. Despite fairly good sales, the company was losing money. The two models produced in 1928, Series 36 and 81, were fine cars, but they were not competitive in cost, style or performance. Again drastic changes were imminent, as they had been ten years earlier. Rumors of merger were substantiated, when Pierce-Arrow did merge with Studebaker in 1928.

Colonel Clifton died June 21, 1928, at seventy-four. Sheppy died in 1927 and was replaced by John Talcott as chief engineer. Also in 1927, Colonel Charles Glidden, the man who had done so much to glorify the Pierce image in the early years, died at seventy. Myron Forbes had breathed new life into the company after the depression of 1921. By the end of 1929, he, too, was gone.

The Pierce-Arrow past had been proud, but now it faced another crisis. And although it still would build some of the best-engineered cars available, it would not be enough to withstand the Depression.

Series 31-51 were made in 1919 and 1920. In this series, the top vents were no longer used. (Courtesy of the Motor Vehicle Manufacturers Association.)

The Series 31-51 Sedan had a new look and was a "transition" style toward the totally different Series 32 look of 1921. (Courtesy of the Motor Vehicle Manufacturers Association.)

FRENCH BROUGHAM   VESTIBULE BROUGHAM

RUNABOUT   VESTIBULE SUBURBAN

Top and center—Most of the models in the Series 31-51 lines are similar to the past five series. (Courtesy of the Motor Vehicle Manufacturers Association.) *Bottom*—Series 31-51 Brougham. (Courtesy of the Motor Vehicle Manufacturers Association.)

By 1921 practically none of the Old Guard was left at Pierce. Postwar change made it a different company, with different management and philosophy. The personal character and ideals of the founders were no longer present at Pierce-Arrow.

INLET SIDE OF MOTOR   EXHAUST SIDE OF MOTOR

Top left and right —The new dual-valve engine with detachable heads used in the Series 31-51 cars (1919–1920). (Courtesy of the Motor Vehicle Manufacturers Association.) *Bottom left* —Colonel George W. Mixter, president of the Pierce-Arrow Motor Car Company, 1920–1921. (Courtesy of the Pierce-Arrow Society.) *Bottom right* —Colonel Clifton in the early 1920s, impeccably dressed as usual. (Courtesy of the University of Michigan.)

This and facing page: Series 32 models for 1921. The bodies with the "new look" had been designed by the Leon Rubay Company of Cleveland. The enclosed cars had "loop" door handles. Factory photos showed "drum" headlights, but most had the usual fender headlights. (Courtesy of the University of Michigan.)

Coupé-Sedan

Vestibule-Sedan

Brougham

Limousine

Sedan

Specifications in Brief of the PIERCE-ARROW CAR

WHEEL BASE	138 inches all models.
TREAD	56 inches.
NUMBER OF CYLINDERS	Six, cast in block.
CYLINDER DIMENSIONS	4 x 5½ inches.
REVOLUTIONS PER MINUTE	200 to 3000.
OILING	Pressure feed to all crank shaft journals and pins, cam shafts, cylinders and pistons.
IGNITION	Pierce-Arrow Delco jump-spark and storage battery—two separate coils. Two separate distributors—two sets of spark plugs operating separately or in unison.
BATTERY EQUIPMENT	Willard storage battery.
GENERATOR	Pierce-Arrow Delco instrument.
STARTING MOTOR	Pierce-Arrow Delco instrument.
CARBURETOR	Pierce-Arrow-Stromberg.
CONTROL	Ignition and throttle levers located on top of steering column. New foot accelerator.
CLUTCH	Multiple disc dry plate.
TRANSMISSION	Selective, sliding gears, direct on high speed with free wheel on second speed.
SPEEDS	Three forward and reverse.
FINAL DRIVE	Spiral bevel gears.
FRONT AXLE	Drop forged, alloy steel, heat-treated I-beam
REAR AXLE	Semi-floating.
STEERING GEAR	Pierce-Arrow screw and nut.
BEARINGS	Ball and roller bearings throughout, except in engine.
BRAKES	Equalized foot brakes on outside of drums on hubs, both rear wheels. Equalized hand brakes on inside of drums on hubs, both rear wheels.
SPRINGS	Front, long semi-elliptic; rear, long semi-elliptic.
WHEELS	Wood, artillery all models.
RIMS	Firestone demountable, with quick, detachable channels.
TIRES	Straight side, option of Goodrich Silvertown Cord, Goodyear Cord of United States Royal Cord.
TIRE DIMENSIONS	35 x 5 inches (actual 36¾ x 5¾ inches) front and rear in all models, except cars of 4-passenger capacity and less, which are equipped with 33 x 5 inches (actual 34½ x 5½ inches).
GASOLINE CAPACITY	26 gallons, all models.
SHOCK ABSORBERS	Gabriel snubbers, front and rear.
LIGHTS	Front, two embodied in crown of fenders on open cars; on brackets on enclosed cars; option either way if specified.
	Dimmers.
	Head lamps fitted with small driving lights for city use.
	Non-glare lenses fitted in head lamps.
	Rear, one combination tail light and number illuminator.

Standard Equipment of all Chassis

Speedometer, odometer, clock.
Shock absorbers on each spring.
Non-glare lenses on head lamps.
Electric horn.
Hand inspection lamp.
Gasoline primer.
Gasoline tank gauge.

Emergency gasoline supply.
Power driven air pump for tires.
Front collision bumper.
Detachable folding trunk rack on all touring models.
Complete set of tools.
Heater in all enclosed cars.

Locks with universal key, on two dash cabinets, tool compartment, tire carrier, ignition and lighting switch and hood over engine.
Alemite grease gun and flexible connection.
Two spare rims.
Slip cover for top on open cars.

Sales specifications for the Series 32 cars (1921). (Courtesy of the Motor Vehicle Manufacturers Association.)

128

Two company publicity photos of Series 32 models. Note the wire wheels—unusual for early Pierce-Arrows. (Courtesy of the Motor Vehicle Manufacturers Association.)

Above—President Coolidge and the White House Series 32 Pierce-Arrow. (Courtesy of the Motor Vehicle Manufacturers Association.) *Below*—A possible transitional or custom rebodied (Series 32) Landaulet on an earlier chassis (circa 1920). (Courtesy of the University of Michigan.)

Top—A 1921 Series 32 Touring with fender headlights. Surviving Series 32 automobiles are rare (four are known). (Courtesy of the Motor Vehicle Manufacturers Association.) *Bottom*—Myron Forbes, president of the Pierce-Arrow Motor Car Company, 1922–1929. He was the "Alfred Sloan" of Pierce-Arrow. (Courtesy of the Pierce-Arrow Society.)

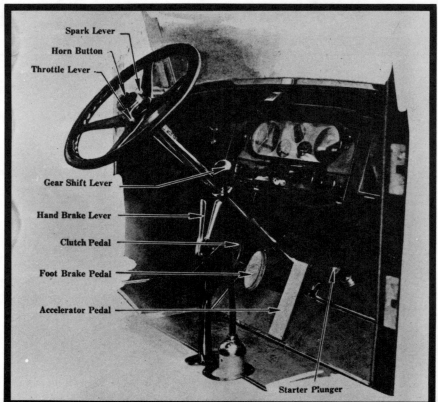

Series 33 instruments. (Courtesy of the Pierce-Arrow Society,)

Top and center—A Series 33 Sedan (1922–1925). External styles were quite similar to that of the previous Series 32. In this series the door handles on the enclosed bodies were the "bar" type. (Courtesy of the Motor Vehicle Manufacturers Association.) *Bottom*—A 1925 photo showing "price cutting" to stimulate sales. Pictured are Series 80 and Series 33 cars in Indiana. What would these cars be worth today? (Courtesy of the Motor Vehicle Manufacturers Association.)

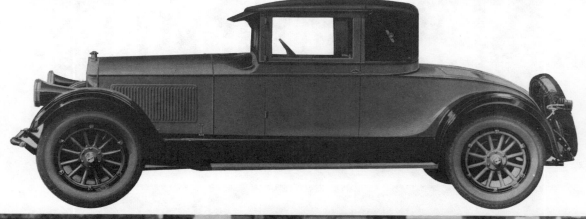

This and facing page: A 1926 Series 80 Runabout, Coupe, five-passenger Coach, seven-passenger Sedan, and enclosed driver Sedan. Hood louvers were different from the previous two series. (Courtesy of the University of Michigan.)

Top—A 1927 Series 80 Landau with a custom body by Brunn. (Courtesy of the Motor Vehicle Manufacturers Association.) *Bottom*—A 1926 publicity photo showing a Series 80 enclosed-driver Sedan. Note the hood ornament with Mercury throwing an arrow. (Courtesy of the University of Michigan.)

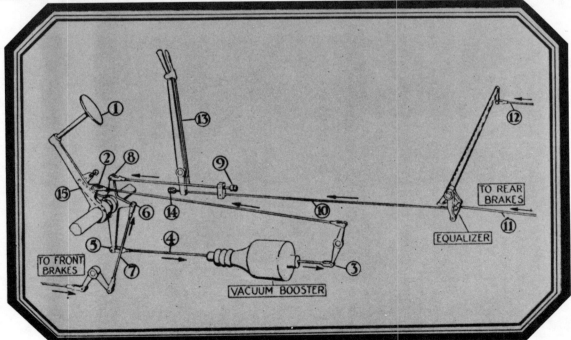

Top—The aluminum Pierce- Arrow with a Pomeroy aluminum engine (circa 1926). Of the
seven cars fabricated, the sole survivor is in Ford's Edison Museum. (Courtesy of the Pierce-Arrow Society.)
Bottom—A schematic of the new four-wheel vacuum-assisted braking system used on Series 36 cars.
(Courtesy of the Pierce-Arrow Society.)

Top and center—A 1927 Series 36 Vestibule Sedan and a Limousine. Series 36 bodies were similar to Series 32 cars at first glance but can be distinguished by their six sets of triple hood louvers. (Courtesy of the Motor Vehicle Manufacturers Association.) *Bottom*—A 1928 series French Landau in the White House fleet of cars. Note the U.S. seal on the rear door. (Courtesy of the Motor Vehicle Manufacturers Association.)

The 1928 Series 81 Runabout and Convertible Coupe. Small unique headlights were used for this one year. (Courtesy of the Motor Vehicle Manufacturers Association.)

Variations on the Series 81 Coupe with and without the rumble seat. Rare drum headlights are shown on these two cars. (Courtesy of the University of Michigan.)

Series 81, four-passenger Coupe Deluxe and two-door Sedan. This series has paired louvers and the helmeted archer appears for the first time as a radiator option. (Courtesy of the University of Michigan.)

Above—Series 81 Club Sedan and five-passenger Sedan. (Courtesy of the University of Michigan.)
Facing page: *Top and center*— Series 81 Enclosed-Driver Limousine and an all-weather Landau. (Courtesy of the University of Michigan.) *Bottom*—The Pierce family crest used on the Series 36 and Series 81 cars in 1928. Unfortunately it was the *wrong* Pierce family, and on 1929 cars it was removed.

The Pierce-Arrow past had been proud, but now it faced another crisis. And although it still would build some of the best-engineered cars available, it would not be enough to withstand the Depression.

Top—Series 81 French Opera Brougham. (Courtesy of the University of Michigan.) *Bottom*—A company photo showing the two types of headlights available. (Courtesy of the University of Michigan.)

7
THE
STUDEBAKER YEARS
1928–33

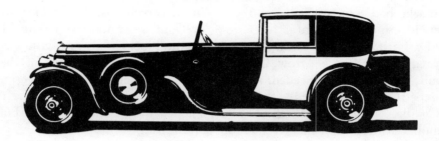

The 1920s had been a volatile era. Prohibition had unsettled the nonteetotaler. The flappers had bloomed. Spending rose at a dizzy pace while fiscal husbandry was repressed. The bubble was about to break in 1929, but even before that Pierce-Arrow was in trouble. During their final ten years, despite periods of high sales, beautiful designs and industry firsts, the company never was able to get completely out of trouble.

Pierce-Arrow was losing money in 1927 and 1928, and drastic changes were again needed. Studebaker was a firm with a history going back to the building of wagons in the mid-nineteenth century. During the 1920s its sales, like so many other companies', were falling, but nevertheless it was a financially solid company. Studebaker did not make an expensive automobile in the Pierce-Arrow class. Thus, a merger could offer symbiotic advantages to both companies. Pierce could use the assets of the profitable Studebaker Company, while Studebaker could round out their line with a prestigious model. Common sales and marketing facilities could also increase efficiency and widen distribution.

After negotiations in early 1928, Studebaker offered to buy Pierce-Arrow stock for $2 million, with the money going to Pierce-Arrow, (money much needed at P-A). When the merger was finally approved by the stockholders on August 7, 1928,

Studebaker bought $5.7 million of Pierce-Arrow stock. Initially, there was resistance at Pierce to the merger, but when the financial picture of increasing losses was presented to the stockholders by President Forbes, it became apparent that they had no choice. The papers were signed August 15, 1928, to make them the fourth largest automobile group, after General Motors, Ford and Chrysler.

Albert Erskine, president of Studebaker, became the chairman of the board of Pierce-Arrow. Erskine was born in 1871 in Huntsville, Alabama. From bookkeeping he progressed to becoming auditor of Yale and Towne Manufacturing Company, vice president of Underwood Typewriter Company and eventually president of Studebaker. Meanwhile Forbes remained president of Pierce. The combined sales forces became the Studebaker–Pierce-Arrow Export Corporation. The two manufacturing operations continued to be completely separate. Pierce-Arrows were still fabricated entirely at Buffalo. The Pierce engine blocks were cast at South Bend, Indiana, but they were not the "reworked" Studebaker blocks that some people have suggested. The composition of the blocks was unique; the Pierce-Arrow engineers still insisted on the highest quality. The Pierce engine blocks were cast of harder material than were the Studebaker blocks. There was naturally an interchange of personnel and ideas between the two companies. Barney

Roos was then chief engineer at Studebaker. He had worked at Pierce-Arrow eight years earlier. The chief engineer at Pierce-Arrow, John Talcott, died in 1928 and was succeeded by Karl M. Wise, who continued as chief engineer during the association with Studebaker. In 1934 Wise was succeeded by LeRoy F. Maurer, who moved up from assistant chief engineer. Charles Pluethner, who had come to Pierce in 1907, remained in the engineering department.

It was agreed by both companies that radical changes were necessary for the Pierce-Arrow. Like ten years earlier, a totally new design was needed. At this time car building expertise had progressed to the point where Packard, Cadillac, Lincoln and others were making fine automobiles. Pierce now had to catch up and surpass those manufacturers with its new line for 1929. There was not much time to develop this all-new model, and the rapidity with which the merged companies accomplished this again leads historians to wonder how much "Studebaker" there was in the 1929 Pierce-Arrow. The new model was brought out in less than half a year! Many insisted that the new Pierce-Arrow was basically a Studebaker President. Actually the work on the new straight eight engine had begun long before the merger with Studebaker, and the new engine was completely a Pierce design. The new car was announced in January 1929, and production of the car apparently ran through 1929 into 1930.

Whatever its lineage, the 1929 design was beautiful and did the trick. The very attractive car brought Pierce-Arrow its most successful production year, with 9,840 cars. Orders for the car poured in, and production could not keep up—a pleasant change, reminiscent of the early years. Although the big depression came in the fall of 1929, its effect on car sales was not felt for a couple of years. The worst year of the depression was 1932.

Models 133 and 143

The 1929 cars came in two models: the 133 (standard line) and the 143 (custom line), which also denoted their respective wheelbases. These chassis were several inches longer than the Series 81 and 36 of the previous year (130″ and 138″ wheelbases respectively). The big change, and probably the main reason for the sales success of that year besides attractive styling, was that Pierce-Arrow finally went to an

eight-cylinder "L" engine. This was a straight eight cast "en block" with a detachable head that used nine main bearings. Bore and stroke was 3½″ x 4¾″, giving a displacement of 366 c. and a compression ratio of 5.1 to 1. At an engine speed of 3,200 rpm (maximum was 3,800 rpm), it could develop 125 b.h.p. A dual updraft carburetor (Stromberg Model UU2) was used in the two chassis. With four forward gears a top speed of 85 miles per hour was obtainable. Interestingly, the engine blocks were cast with a code in the block to specify the day and hour of the casting. This enabled the metallurgists to keep much better quality control on the iron used. The rough castings were shipped from South Bend to Buffalo for machining and finishing.

The straight eight was probably one of the best all-around engines that Pierce ever built. The later V-12 was a magnificent piece of machinery, but the straight eight was cheaper to produce and was what the company really needed during the depression years. Actually, the company would have been way ahead if they had gone to the eight-cylinder engine in 1927 and 1928 instead of continuing with outmoded designs of the Series 36 and 81.

The many body styles available still held onto traditional Pierce-Arrow quality, with walnut garnish moldings, silk curtains and vanities in the rear. Styles in the Model 133, with their prices, were:

Roadster	$2,875
Sedan	$2,975
Brougham	$2,775
Sedan-Seven-Passenger	$2,150
Touring	$2,975
Coupe	$2,975
Town Sedan	$3,150
Enclosed-Driver Limousine	$3,350
Sport Phaeton	$3,150
Deluxe Sedan	$3,350
Deluxe Club Sedan	$3,490
Tonneau Cowl Phaeton	$3,325

Styles found in Model 144 were:

Seven-Passenger Touring	$3,750
Five-Passenger Sedan	$3,975
Convertible Coupe	$3,750
Enclosed-Driver Limousine	$4,250

All-Weather Sedan	$5,750
All-Weather Brougham	$7,500
French Brougham	$8,200

Fafnir ball-bearing spring shackles were used on all models after January 1929. Each car had twelve shackles, greased and sealed at the factory to prevent leaking. Shatterproof glass from Pittsburgh Plate Glass, developed in 1926, was first used in this year's models. Wooden wheels were standard, but wire wheels were available and often used in company advertising photos. Opening the lacquered radiator louvers was automatically controlled by the water temperature. The design of the 1929 models was vastly superior to the previous Series 36 and 81.

At the beginning of the fourth quarter of 1929, some changes were made in the 133 line of cars. Because of sales pressure from competition, late 1929 models were registered as 1930 cars, although production of the true 1930 models A, B, and C was not actually begun until the first of 1930. As a result, there seemed to be a disagreement whether the cars made in late 1929 should really be considered 1929 or 1930 cars. At this point in time it probably does not make much difference. The only accurate method of identifying the year is by the serial number on the frame-mounted serial number plate.

In December 1929, President Forbes, who had done so much for Pierce-Arrow, resigned. He was replaced by Albert Erskine. Arthur J. Chanter transferred from Studebaker to become the new vice president of Pierce-Arrow. By 1930 financial prospects at Pierce looked quite encouraging.

1930 Models A, B, C

Although the depression worsened, business at Pierce remained relatively good; the year 1930 was its second largest manufacturing year, with 6,916 units produced. Although the external appearance of the 1930 models changed little from the previous year, the chassis were new. Four different wheelbases were available instead of two. Elated over the best year in sales, Pierce fell into its old pattern of producing too many variations—a poor decision in the face of a deepening Depression.

Three models were made: Model A (144" wheelbase); Model B (134" or 139" wheelbase); and Model C (132" wheelbase). Production was begun in January

1930. A total of eighteen standard styles were available with prices ranging from $2,775 to $8,200 (that's a lot of five-cent apples).

Model A, 144" Wheelbase
Seven-Passenger Touring
Convertible Coupe
Seven-Passenger Sedan
Seven-Passenger Enclosed-Driver Limousine
Town Car

Model B, 134" Wheelbase
Roadster with Rumble Seat
Dual-Cowl Phaeton
Four-Passenger Touring
Convertible Coupe

Model B, 139" Wheelbase
Five-Passenger Sedan
Club Sedan
Club Berline
Victoria
Seven-Passenger Enclosed-Driver Limousine

Model C, 132" Wheelbase
Coupe with Rumble Seat
Five-Passenger Club Brougham
Five-Passenger Sedan

Each model had a different displacement engine but used the same basic block.

Model A—385 CID (3½x x 5"), 132 HP
Model B—366 CID (3½" x 4¾"), 125 HP
Model C—340 CID (3⅜" x 4¾"), 115 HP

There appears to be needless extra production cost for little practical difference in power. Available rear-end ratios were 4.08, 4.42 (standard), and 4.58 to 1. The cheaper Model C was in effect a modified 1929 standard 133 model. It retained the old single-belt fan, while Models A and B used the new dual "V"-belt fan. In addition, the larger models used 18" x 7" tires, while the Model C used 19" x 6.50". The twelve-hickory-spoke wooden artillery wheels were still standard, while wire wheels were optional at extra cost. The grouped narrow-hood louvers from 1929 (still found on the 1930 Model C) were replaced by a five-hinged door on the Models A and B. A few late-model 1929 cars also came with hood doors.

Thirty-two standard color options were offered, with many upholstery combinations; as usual any option was available at a price.

An example is the 1930 Brunn-bodied custom Pierce-Arrow Limousine made for Riza Khan, the Shah of Persia. George H. Woodfield, who had been employed by Brunn and Company but loaned to Studebaker, designed this custom automobile with gold-plated hardware, champagne-colored silk upholstery, inlaid satin wood trim and wolfhound fur rugs on the floor—Rolls-Royce, eat your heart out. This car received considerable notoriety and was on display in New York City. At $30,000 it was the most expensive car that Pierce-Arrow ever made. At last word this car still exists in Tehran. Originally white it now has been repainted deep blue.

Cadillac introduced its V-16 engine in 1930. It was smooth, powerful and impressive. Packard had been building the "Twin-Six" for a number of years. Packard and Lincoln both introduced their new V-12 engines in 1932. The multicylinder race had been going on for some time, and despite Pierce's change to the straight eight in 1929, the company was still psychologically behind. When the Cadillac V-16 appeared, the Pierce engineering department, under Karl Wise, began to work on a Pierce V-12, but this new engine was not introduced until November 1931.

A second run of cars was produced beginning in mid-1930. These were modified by adding deluxe options, such as double bumpers, twin horns, and more chrome. The over-zealous sales department called these 1931 models. Actually all of the cars made by Pierce during 1929, 1930 and 1931 look very similar, and it is difficult at first glance to be sure just which model is which. When in doubt, check the serial number and engine number.

1931
Models 41, 42 and 43

In January 1931 the new Models 41, 42 and 43 were introduced. Although the chassis were larger than those of 1930, the external appearance was changed little. The wheelbases were extended about 3 inches to 147 inches, 142 inches, and 134 inches or 137 inches respectively for the three models. After the small 130-inch wheelbase chassis of the Series 80, Pierce-Arrow's heritage drew it inexorably back to the larger cars. Prices ranged from $2,695 to $6,250,

slightly lower than those of 1930.

The two larger models, 41 and 42, used the larger 385 CID engine (132 horsepower). Model 43 used the 125-horsepower 366 CID engine, while the old 115-horsepower 340 CID engine was discontinued. The Bendix duo-servo mechanical brakes were still in use, and they were quite adequate. A four-speed transmission made by Clark Equipment Company was used.

In 1931 a chrome-plated or painted-metal side-mount tire cover was available in addition to the canvas covers of previous years. A variety of wheel-cover options was offered from 1930 through 1932. Another distinguishing feature was the bumper; the 1930 cars had two narrow bumpers, and the 1931 models wide bumpers with very little space between them. The one exception was the larger Model 41, which carried a wide, single bumper characteristic of all 1932 models. The splash pans were noticeably narrower than those of the previous year.

A new feature in 1931 was a freewheeling device, which could be engaged or disengaged by a dash-mounted lever. Now illegal, it was thought to offer better fuel economy and a smoother ride. It came on all models produced through 1935.

During the early 1930s, Pierce-Arrow made a beautiful and finely-tuned car. Pierce-Arrow engines frequently were the first choice of illegal rum runners because of their characteristically quiet engines. However, sales decreased with the worsening Depression. Car prices were reduced each year to stimulate sales, but to little avail.

The Pierce-Arrow Company of Canada was organized at the end of 1931. Automobile components were not manufactured there but merely assembled from parts shipped by the Buffalo plant. This plant in Walkerville, Ontario, belonged to Studebaker. Although the Pierce-Arrow–Studebaker merger dissolved in 1933, car assembly at Walkerville continued through 1935. The total output during those four years was only 189 units. Studebaker then sold the plant in May 1936.

It is interesting to note the ads that Pierce-Arrow used during this period. Still artists' drawings rather than photographs, they commonly included small ads from previous years. This referral to the Pierce-Arrow of bygone days was obviously an attempt to hold onto the past "carriage trade" image. Other ads inserted testimonials from prominent people. It is sad to watch the once proud company struggling for survival. Its dedication to making the finest car possible was insufficient to carry the firm through the Depression. Had the company gone to the eight-cylinder engine a few years earlier, it might have survived.

Radiator Ornaments

For many years after automobiles began filling the roads, the radiators were covered with plain brass or hard-rubber caps. The temperature-indicating motometer was introduced in 1912 by Boyce. One could obtain a motometer with the make of the car printed on the circular plate, so that the owner could dress up his pride and joy. These motometers became tremendously popular; they were also quite important to proper care of the engine.

About 1915 Pierce owners could obtain a fancy nickeled radiator ornament shaped like a wheel pierced with an arrow. Through the next ten years slight variations occurred in this design. Custom-made caps were not unusual. The White House Pierce-Arrow carried an eagle with spread wings on its radiator. In the 1920s an unusual ornament of Mercury throwing an arrow was found on some Pierces. A hexagon containing a Model 80 Pierce front-end also appeared during the mid-1920s.

During the 1920s more prestige cars had the option of a special radiator ornament which could be identified with their cars. Rolls-Royce led the way with their "Spirit of Ecstasy" in 1912. Packard had "Daphne at the Well"; Cadillac had the "Trumpeter"; and Hispano-Suiza their "Stork."

In 1928, owners of Series 36 or 81 cars had the option of a helmeted archer to adorn their radiator cap. Like the option of fender headlamps, which subtly connoted Pierce-Arrow ownership, the archer quickly became associated with the Pierce-Arrow. Unfortunately these were readily accessible to art collectors, and frequently were "lost." Today the archer is quite a collectible and is guarded by car owners. Later-model Pierce-Arrows had the archers attached by a chain inside the radiator neck, and in the last cars they were permanently attached to the radiator shell.

In the spring of 1930, Pierce-Arrow decided to restyle the archer to make it more aesthetically appealing. The assignment was given to General Motors' Ternstedt division, which made automobile hardware.

William N. Schnell was responsible for the design, along with Bonnie Lemm (designer), Frederick Tuntinne (sculpturer), and Al Gonas (who posed for the archer). The working drawings were completed in December 1930. The new "bareheaded archer" became available as an option on the 1931 Pierce-Arrows. The name Schnell is found imprinted on the base of the original archers. This beautiful ornament became quite popular and was added regularly by Pierce owners. Until 1933 only Turnstedt made the archer. After that other companies (Doehler-Jarvis, Stant, etc.) produced them. In 1933 the archer was cast with the figure and base as one piece. From 1934 on, the archer was mounted to an arrow-shaped base, which in turn was attached to the grill shell by a hidden metal tongue. At the rear of the hood hinge was a plate in the shape of tail feathers. Thus, viewed from above, the archer base, hood hinge, and plate formed a complete arrow.

Today in the antique-car hobby the Pierce-Arrow archer still remains one of the most beautiful and sought-after of the ornaments.

1932
Models 51, 52, 53, and 54

The big news at Pierce in 1932 was the introduction of the new V-12 engine on November 9, 1931. Competition had forced them to make this move. The engine design was begun a couple of years earlier. The V-12 engine was used in the two larger chassis (142″ and 147″) of the four models produced, but it was also available in the 137″ chassis, if ordered.

Model	Wheelbase	Bore and Stroke	HP and RPM	CID
51	147″	3⅜″ x 4″	150 @ 3,200	429
52	147″	3⅜″ x 4″	150 @ 3,200	429
53	142-137″	3¼″ x 4″	140 @ 3,200	398
54	142-137″ (8-cylinder)	3½″ x 4¾″	125 @ 3,800	366

The V-12 engine was mounted on eight rubber supports. The two banks of cylinders were included at an unusual 80-degree angle.

The engine had a 5.05 to 1 compression ratio and did not require antiknock fuel. The synchromesh transmission connected to three forward gears, with free-wheeling. The wheel tread was increased to 61½ inches. The standard 18-inch wood artillery wheel could be replaced by the optional wire wheels or Budd steel artillery wheels, with lacquer or natural wood finish.

The Startix automatic starter was standard on the 1932 Pierce-Arrows (as well as on other prestige American cars). The ride-control shock absorbers were regulated by a dash-mounted lever, beside the free-wheeling lever.

Commercial radio first appeared in 1920 with station KDK in Pittsburgh. In 1932 Pierce automobiles had antennae available for those cars containing steering-column-mounted Philco radios. In an age of transistors one forgets that the listener had to wait interminably for the tubes to warm up.

The body styles for 1932 were similar to those of the previous three years, but they were more flowing and less "boxy." The author thinks that the 1932 models were the prettiest that Pierce ever made. The windshield was sloped to give it a racy appearance, and a V-shaped radiator shell was characteristic for that year. All models carried the single curved bumpers. Twelve standard body styles were available.

LeBaron made five body styles for the 1932 chassis. A company brochure also shows a line of five custom-bodied town cars by Brunn and Company of Buffalo.

The Flight of the Arrow

The V-12 engine was a smooth-running, beautiful piece of equipment. It was powerful enough to accelerate smartly the large 5,500-pound chassis. The cars could cruise comfortably at 80 miles per hour. Now that Pierce had the engine, it needed publicity. This responsibility was given to Pierce-Arrow Engineer Omar J. Diles. He arranged a demonstration of the V-12 engine's performance and dependability. Ab Jenkins, a Mormon from Utah, was selected to drive the car. Jenkins had been a competition driver for Studebaker and later a test driver for Pierce.

A twenty-four-hour endurance run was planned on a ten-mile circular track laid out on the Bonneville Salt Flats. Due to hurried arrangements, the AAA was not able to supervise this run and make it official. The car used was a 1932 Roadster chassis with the fenders removed. It was powered by a souped-up 1933 V-12 engine that previously had been tested for 151 hours on a dynamometer at 4,000 rpm.

On September 18, 1932, Jenkins drove alone for twenty-four hours. He covered 271 laps for a distance of 2,710 miles at an average speed of 112.91 miles per hour. The car performed flawlessly, and only twelve pit stops were made for gas and oil. The four Firestone tires never needed changing. Later in 1932 Jenkins toured the country with films of the event to publicize the new Pierce V-12 engine.

Spurred on by success of the run, Pierce planned a

Models and Prices

Body Type	Model 54*	Model 53**	Model 52†
Club Brougham, Five-Passenger	$2,385	$3,185	—
Club Sedan, Five-Passenger	$2,650	$3,450	$3,885
Sedan, Five-Passenger	$2,458	$3,285	$3,785
Club Berline, Five-Passenger	$2,850	$3,650	$4,085
Convertible Sedan, Five-Passenger	$2,950	$3,750	—
Sedan, Seven-Passenger	$2,750	$3,550	$4,085
Enclosed-Drive Limousine, Seven-Passenger	$2,950	$3,750	$4,250
Coupe, Four-Passenger	$2,485	$3,285	—
Convertible Coupe Roadster, Four-Passenger	$2,650	$3,450	—
Tourer, Five-Passenger	$2,750	$3,550	—
Tourer, Seven-Passenger	$2,850	$3,650	—
Sport Phaeton, Five-Passenger	$3,050	$3,850	—

*8-cylinder, 137"–142" wheelbase.
**12-cylinder, 137"–142" wheelbase.
†12-cylinder, 142"–147" wheelbase.

1933 Bonneville run. This time the company went after speed records, with the AAA there to sanction and conduct the event. Omar Diles again was the Pierce engineer in charge, and Ab Jenkins the driver. The car was a stripped 1933 Convertible V-12. The engine had been modified to develop 207 horsepower with 7.5 to 1 compression. On August 6, 133, Jenkins drove for twenty-five and one-half hours. He averaged 117 miles per hour for 3,000 miles. The trial broke sixty-six official AAA records. A movie "The Flight of the Arrow" was made of this run, and it was shown around the country as promotional material. To demonstrate what a great road car Pierce-Arrow had, and to show Ab Jenkins' derring-do, he shaved his face with a safety razor while driving at 125 miles per hour.

In August, 1934, a third twenty-four-hour record run was held, and Jenkins set a new world's record of 127 miles per hour average in a twenty-four-hour period.

Despite impressive records and beautifully-designed automobiles, sales dropped with the worsening Depression. Pierce had spent about $2 million between 1930 and 1932 on factory improvements, (probably because of the encouraging sales of 1929). In 1932, with sales of $8 million, the company still lost $3 million! Pierce raised the average price of its cars about $500 that year. It did not bring in enough additional money, and it probably drove buyers away in that bleak year. Despite extensive advertising only 2,692 cars sold in 1932, a 25 per cent drop from the previous year's sales.

Roy Faulkner, who had been president of Auburn, was put in charge of Pierce-Arrow sales in October 1932. This caused speculation that Pierce-Arrow might merge with Auburn. He was responsible for Ab Jenkins's assault on the world speed records, and for the Silver Arrow of 1933 (Chapter 8). Although he spurred a brief increase in sales with the V-12 promotion, Faulkner left Pierce in September 1934 and returned to Auburn.

Studebaker and Pierce-Arrow Split

The beautiful new cars of 1929 through 1932 were readily-accepted by the buying public, with good sales during the first part of this period. The management at Pierce became overly optimistic and did not correctly anticipate the worsening effect of the Depression. The considerable sum of money spent on factory improvements would have been better saved. The judgment of Studebaker's management was equally faulty. Studebaker had been subsidizing Pierce losses during this period. It also overextended itself in purchasing the White Motor Corporation. Later the White Motor Corporation would continue to build Pierce trucks after Pierce-Arrow stopped its production (Chapter 9).

In the spring of 1933 Studebaker went bankrupt and into receivership. Since Pierce-Arrow had borrowed money from Studebaker, Studebaker creditors tried unsuccessfully to get money from Pierce-Arrow. Pierce-Arrow once had been a family business in Buffalo, and on August 26, 1933, Studebaker sold Pierce-Arrow to a group of Buffalo businessmen for $1 million. The money was given to Studebaker to help pay off its creditors, and the rest of Pierce-Arrow's debt to Studebaker was cancelled.

After Studebaker's bankruptcy, the receivers forced the resignation of President Albert Erskine. In July, 1933, he committed suicide. Arthur J. Chanter was made president of Pierce-Arrow in April 1933. He had been with Studebaker for many years, starting as a test driver, and had become vice president of Pierce-Arrow in 1928. Roy Faulkner moved up from sales to vice president of Pierce-Arrow.

With increased advertising and publicity, sales did show a temporary increase in early 1933. Unfortunately, a Detroit tool and die makers' strike hurt Pierce production during mid-1933. Again, sales that year dropped from 1932. Only 2,152 cars were produced in 1933.

In August 1933, after five years of association with Studebaker, Pierce-Arrow once again became a privately-owned company. During those five years Pierce had produced some of its handsomest cars, and sales had hit an all-time high in 1929. Pierce-Arrow cars had broken speed records. Two well-designed and beautifully-running engines that were as good as any engine of that period had been developed, and hydraulic tappets had been introduced. Despite all this sales fell, and the company began its inexorable decline. Even this company, dedicated to the highest quality, could not endure a prolonged Depression. Pierce-Arrow found itself with a stigma of failure, difficult to shake.

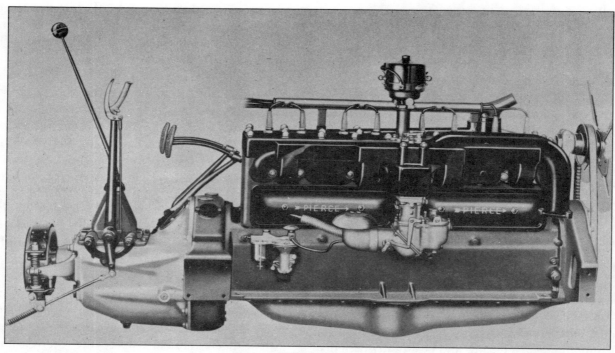

B. H. Warner
Manufacturing

Albert R.
Erskine
President

Arthur J. Chanter
Vice-President

Karl M. Wise, Engineering

George E. Willis, Sales

Top—The new eight-cylinder "L" type engine brought out in 1929. It delivered 125 horsepower at 3,200 rpm. (Courtesy of the Motor Vehicle Manufacturers Association.) *Bottom*—The Pierce-Arrow officers as pictured in a 1930 company promotional publication. (Courtesy of the Pierce-Arrow Society.)

The 1929 Models 133 and 143. The Model 133 cars had small hood louvers arranged in seven groups of three. The larger Model 143 cars had movable doors. (Courtesy of the Pierce-Arrow Society.)

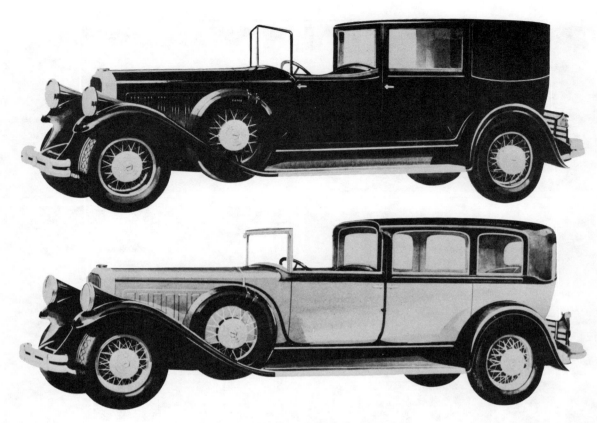

Top and center—Two 1929 custom-bodied Pierce-Arrows: A Willowghby Town Car and a Holbrook Opera Brougham. Were these cars actually made? (Courtesy of the Motor Vehicle Manufacturers Association.) *Bottom*—The new Fafnir ball bearing spring shackles. (Courtesy of the Pierce-Arrow Society.)

The 1930 Group A Models with 144-inch wheel base: Convertible Coupe, Touring, seven-passenger Sedan, and All-Weather Town Car. (Courtesy of the University of Michigan.)

. . . Pierce fell into its old pattern of producing too many variations—a poor decision in the face of a deepening Depression.

Two of the 1930 Group B models with 134-inch wheelbase: Sport Roadster and Sport Phaeton. (Courtesy of the Motor Vehicle Manufacturers Association.)

A total of eighteen standard styles were available with prices ranging from $2,775 to $8,200 (that's a lot of five-cent apples).

The other 1930 Group B models with 134-inch wheelbase: Club Sedan and seven-passenger Sedan. (Courtesy of the Motor Vehicle Manufacturers Association.)

Top—A 1930 artist's sketch used in advertisements. (Courtesy of the University of Michigan.)
Bottom—The less expensive Model C of 1930 looked like the 1929 models, retaining louvers instead of hood doors. (Courtesy of the University of Michigan.)

". . . this custom automobile with gold-plated hardware, champagne-colored silk upholstery, inlaid satin wood trim and wolfhound fur rugs on the floor—Rolls-Royce, eat your heart out."

The 1930 Brunn-bodied Limousine designed by George Woodfield for the Shah of Persia. At $30,000 this was the most expensive car that Pierce-Arrow ever made. (Courtesy of the Motor Vehicle Manufacturers Association.)

A 1931 Model 41 Convertible Coupe (with single bumper), Model 42 Touring (with double bumper), and a seven-passenger Sedan. Note the narrower splash pans in the 1931 models. (Courtesy of the Motor Vehicle Manufacturers Association.)

Top—A beautiful 1931 Victoria Coupe by LeBaron. (Courtesy of the Motor Vehicle Manufacturers Association.) *Center and bottom*—The 1931 Town Car that was displayed as the New York show car. This one-off Model 41 is presently owned by Gordon Tucker. (Courtesy of the Motor Vehicle Manufacturers Association.)

Top—A 1931 Convertible Coupe by Waterhouse. (Courtesy of the Motor Vehicle Manufacturers Association.)
Center and bottom—Proposed 1931 Models by Hibbard and Darrin. It is questionable whether these cars were ever built. (Courtesy of the Motor Vehicle Manufacturers Association.)

A typical advertisement of the early 1930s with an insert recalling traditional
Pierce-Arrow quality. (Author's collection.)

Top left—A Boyce motometer of the mid-teens (on a 1913 Pierce-Arrow). *Top right*—The Pierce-Arrow radiator ornament generally available from about 1915 until 1928. *Bottom left*—A variation of the postwar ornament. *Bottom right*—A Pierce-Arrow ornament from the mid-1920s.

Top—A model of an early helmeted archer, designed by Herbert Dawley (a forerunner of the 1928 archer). (Courtesy of the Pierce-Arrow Society.) *Bottom*—The helmeted archer first available as an option on the Series 81 cars of 1928.

Top—The archer was permanently attached to the radiator shell from 1934 to 1938. The radiator nozzle was concealed under the hood. *Bottom*—The beautiful bare-headed archer first appeared on the 1931 models. This is one of the ornaments most sought after by collectors.

Top—A 1932 Club Sedan shown with a 1901 Motorette. (Courtesy of the Motor Vehicle Manufacturers Association.) *Bottom*—A 1932 five-passenger Sedan. (Courtesy of the Motor Vehicle Manufacturers Association.)

The 1932 Club Brougham and Club Berline. The single bumper was standard in 1932. (Courtesy of the Motor Vehicle Manufacturers Association.)

The 1932 Convertible Coupe Roadster and Coupe. (Courtesy of the University of Michigan.)

The 1932 Sport Phaeton and Convertible Sedan. (Courtesy of the University of Michigan.)

A 1932 LeBaron Close-Coupled Sedan (with rare "V" windshield) and LeBaron Coupe. (Courtesy of the Motor Vehicle Manufacturers Association.)

Top—The new 1932 V-12 engine developing 150 horsepower at 3,200 rpm. It was an excellent engine even by today's standards. The 1903 6-horsepower Pierce engine is shown in comparison. (Courtesy of the Motor Vehicle Manufacturers Association.) *Bottom*—Ab Jenkins, who broke world speed records in 1932, 1933, and 1934, driving a V-12 Pierce-Arrow. (Reprint from *The Flight of the Arrow.*)

Top—Jenkins in the 1933 Model V-12 Roadster (September 18, 1932). (From *The Flight of the Arrow.*)
Bottom—Jenkins at 112.9 mph (From *The Flight of the Arrow.*)

8
THE
SILVER ARROW
1933–38

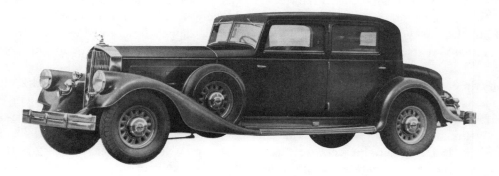

In the early 1930s, the United States government was trying to work its way out of the Depression. Pierce-Arrow was trying to keep the wolf from its door. Ab Jenkins's feat had been a shot in the arm, and with the company's excellent V-12 engine, it could again hold up its head among multicylinder competitors. Still, it needed something to really catch the eye and ignite the enthusiasm of auto buyers. That something came in the form of the inspired Silver Arrow.

When Roy Faulkner arrived at Pierce-Arrow from Auburn, he directed his sales promotional efforts towards the speed record of Ab Jenkins and the design of a revolutionary new Pierce-Arrow. The design of the Silver Arrow was the brainchild of Phil Wright, and it incorporated many automobile firsts. Originally the plan called for a rear-engine chassis, but this turned out to be impractical, so a modified standard chassis was used. The Silver Arrow had an all-steel roof. The flat sides covered the concealed sidemounts and the running boards. The heavy, one-foot-thick doors had recessed door handles. The trunk was integral with the fastback body. The Pierce type radiator matched beautifully the rest of the aerodynamic body. The triangular rear windows were curiously small. The flowing body line had to be broken by the rear window, to gain more headroom for the rear passengers. The interior was, of course, finished with traditional Pierce-Arrow elegance.

Underneath the radical body was the essentially standard 139″ Model 1236 chassis with a 175-horsepower V-12 engine. The weight was 5,729 pounds, making it a little heavier than standard sedans.

The saga of the design and construction of the five show-model Silver Arrows is almost unbelievable. It was decided in the fall of 1932 to build and show the first car at the New York Automobile Show on January 1, 1933—a seemingly impossible deadline of three months. Because larger facilities were available at Studebaker, it was decided to build all five models there, rather than at Buffalo. Paul J. Aumann was to supervise the construction. The men who were to design and build the prototype were hand-picked for their abilities, and work was carried out around the clock in shifts. The gigantic project was accomplished through an esprit de corps typical of the Pierce "family" tradition.

Special engine numbers were set aside for these five cars (360,001–360,011). The first car went to New York City as scheduled in January 1933. The second went to Buffalo in mid-January. The third went to Chicago at the end of January. Cars four and five went to Buffalo in mid-February. The cars were to sell for $10,000, a fraction of their present value. Four of the cars survive; the Pierce-Arrow Society lists cars 003, 005, and 007. One of these was later rebodied as a roadster and became part of Harrah's Automobile Collection. Any person coming up with the fifth car would be quite fortunate. It was probably destroyed.

The Silver Arrow shocked the automobile world and set a standard copied by other manufacturers in later years. Despite its impact on the automobile world, no more cars were made after the initial five. A "production" Silver Arrow was made on a limited scale in 1934 and 1935. Avon even put out an aftershave decanter many years later in the form of the Silver Arrow.

In one year's time, Pierce-Arrow had accomplished some amazing feats. Nevertheless, after a brief surge in sales in early 1933 (Roosevelt had just become president), sales continued to dwindle. Only 2,152 cars were fabricated in 1933. When Pierce-Arrow reorganized after its purchase by independent businessmen in August 1933 it estimated that it could make a profit on the sale of a mere 3,000 cars per year. But even this could not be brought about, despite extensive advertising in magazines.

1933
Models 836 (839), 1236 (1239), 1242, and 1247
The standard cars in 1933 were slightly more streamlined than those of 1932, and were quite attractive. The headlights had a curve continuous with the line of the fender. This reversed curvature was reminiscent of the shape that first appeared in 1914. The V-shaped radiator had a more sloping front, which gave the car a very streamlined appearance. The year 1933 probably represents the last year of the "classic" look at Pierce-Arrow. The 836 and 839 models (both classified as an 836 model) were on 136" and 139" bases. They both had the 366 CID eight-cylinder engine which developed 135 horsepower at 3,400 rpm (3½" x 4¾"). The compression ratio was 5.5 to 1.

The 1236 (1239), 1242 and 1247 models used larger chassis of 136" (or 139"), 137" (or 142"), and 147" wheelbases. These all were powered by V-12 engines. The smaller cars had 429 CID (3⅜" x 4") engines with 160 horsepower at 3,400 rpm, while the larger chassis had the 462 CID (3½" x 4") engines with 175 horsepower at 3,400 rpm. All of this year's engines had more power than in 1932. This was accomplished with the use of a larger fuel manifold, a new dual downdraft carburetor and a higher compression ratio of 6 to 1.

An industry first was introduction of successful hydraulic tappets, which appeared on the 1933 engines. Inventors had tried to perfect a hydraulic tappet since early in the twentieth century, but none worked well or for long. Carl Voorhies, of Pierce-Arrow, developed and patented the self-adjusting hydraulic tappet in 1932. The 1933 models, which came out in November 1932, utilized this innovation. These hydraulic tappets functioned well due to close tolerances of machining (.0002) and constant control of the oil used in them. A full-flow oil cleaner and temperature regulator (temperature exchanged with engine cooling water) was used in the oil system. Voorhies later left Pierce-Arrow for Willcox-Rich and Eaton.

Another new feature on the 1933 models was the Stewart-Warner power brakes. In this system the brake pedal had only a two-inch travel and did not apply any pressure directly to the four-wheel mechanical brakes. All of the power was derived from the rotation of the drive shaft and applied through cables to the four brake shoes. The power was controlled, however, by the brake pedal. This system was similar to that used by Rolls-Royce and other European automobile manufacturers. No other American-built car used this system.

Other features in 1933 were tinted safety glass, cross-beam headlights, automatic choke, synchromesh transmission, freewheeling, adjustable steering column, and an archer radiator emblem (standard on the deluxe models, and a $25 option on regular models). The wheel size was reduced one inch to 17 inches, with steel artillery or wire wheels available. The weight of the various models ranged from 4,618 pounds to 5,778 pounds. Despite its continuing financial battle, Pierce-Arrow made one of the finest cars in America. Interestingly, a 1933 brochure states: "So quiet are the 1933 Pierce-Arrows that driving along the highway, the most noticeable noise is the ticking of the clock." Rolls-Royce "borrowed" that phrase later. In driving a Pierce and a Rolls, one is struck by the difference in ride, however. The author's 1935 Rolls-Royce was quite inferior to his 1932 Pierce-Arrow.

With available chassis wheelbases of 136 inches, 137 inches, 139 inches, 142 inches, and 147 inches, and with combinations of seventeen styles, Pierce was obviously overextending itself again in light of its financial problems. Because of good sales in the early

1930s, world speed records, industry firsts, and the revolutionary Silver-Arrow, perhaps there was some cause for optimism in 1933. Even though Studebaker went into receivership in April of that year, the Pierce management felt a renewed hope and enthusiasm in its reorganization.

The 136-inch and 139-inch-wheelbase models retained the single bumper used in 1932. The 1242 and 1247 models sported a double bumper similar to the 1931 style. Variations and customizing make it difficult to say with authority what is "correct." LeBaron again offered a line of several custom bodies. Their split-"V" windshield was an attractive characteristic.

As 1933 ended, Pierce-Arrow, undaunted by slipping sales, prepared to garner a larger share of the prestige car market. Transient successes coupled with their old naiveté led it to prepare a new line of cars for 1934. In early 1934 the tool and die makers' strike was still affecting production, but the company remained enthusiastic and invested heavily in advertising and promotion. The most-publicized model was the new Production Silver Arrow. This was modeled after the Silver Arrow of 1933, but really was just a streamlined standard model since it did not have the revolutionary features of the famous Silver Arrow: slab side, hidden sidemount tires, rear fender skirts, "V" windshields, etc. The Production Silver Arrow came on a 144-inch-wheelbase chassis with either the 140 horsepower eight-cylinder or 175 horsepower V-12 engine. The number made was limited, and less than a dozen survive. The weight was a little over 2½ tons, and the Depression price tag ranged from $3,500 to $3,900.

1934

Models 836A, 840A, 1240A, and 1248A

In January 1934, three models were introduced: the 840A, 1240A, and 1248A. The 840A carried a 139-inch or 144-inch wheelbase with 385 CID eight-cylinder engine (3½" x 5") developing 140 horsepower at 3,400 rpm. Maximum road speed was about 70 miles per hour. The 17-inch wheel was again used; it was not changed while the company continued to make automobiles. Ten body styles were available. A similar version, but with V-12 engine on the 139-inch or 144-inch wheelbase chassis, was the model 1240A. This twelve-cylinder engine had a 462 CID and developed 175 horsepower at 3,400 rpm. Nine body styles were made. The model 1248A was similar, but

the wheelbase was stretched to 147 inches in this custom line. Again, fine custom Brunn bodies were available.

All body styles were more rounded this year and were losing the classic look. The triple taillight, which had been used since 1925, was replaced by a light integrated into the curve of the fender. This style was used on all of the remaining models through 1938. The archer was now permanently mounted on the painted radiator shell. Only the front grill was chrome, while the radiator shell was painted. Factory photographs show the hood with two horizontal doors. Cars in following years all had three hood doors trimmed with chrome mouldings. A new and different bumper appeared in 1934, dipping in the middle to form a "V."

Later in April 1934 a cheaper model was introduced, the 836A. Like the previous Series 80, it was to offer a Pierce-Arrow within reach of more wallets, and it was designed to boost sales. This 836A had a 366 CID, eight-cylinder engine (3½" x 4¾") with 135 horsepower on a 136-inch chassis. The announcement by Roy Faulkner told of the "really true Pierce-Arrow" at a starting price of only $2,195. This model did not even carry an archer. The radiator shell was rather unattractively altered. Only two styles were available, selling between $2,195 and $2,395 (no, the seats were not extra!). These were the two-door Club Brougham and four-door Sedan. The 836A models can be recognized by the curved-front single bumper, the hood without louvers, the unique radiator grill containing four horizontal chrome strips, and the absence of thermostatically controlled shutters. The number produced was rather limited. It was sad to see the proud company struggling for survival.

One crisis was solved only to have another take its place. In 1934 a national dealer code limiting dealer allowances on used cars went into effect. Since dealers received cars at discounted prices, they utilized the trade-in allowance to control customer cost, dealer profit, and the attractiveness of the "deal." This ruling further hurt dealer sales. After 1933, the company held a steadily downhill course. In 1934, only 1,740 units were manufactured.

By mid-1934 the company had lost about three-quarters of a million dollars and was in receivership. The directors had sought a $1.5 million loan that spring from the Reconstruction Finance Corporation, but due to RFC regulations regarding companies in receivership, the loan was not granted. The company tried to mortgage its physical plant to raise money, and stalled for time until financial help arrived. It never came.

By August the company again went bankrupt, and the RFC loan was lost forever. Efforts were made to merge with Auburn and Reo, but this never materialized.

In the fall, Roy Faulkner left Pierce-Arrow and returned to Auburn, another sinking ship. In desperation, President Chanter appealed to local banks (the Federal Reserve Bank of New York and the Marine Trust Company) and raised a million dollars. George Rand, who founded the Marine Midland Bank in New York, once had been on the Pierce-Arrow Board of Directors.

With the money came the condition of major reorganization of the company. The company actually had been two businesses: the Pierce-Arrow Motor Car Company, which built the cars; and the Pierce-Arrow Sales Corporation, which sold the cars. The financial statements had always been combined. The condition of reorganization was the sale of the Pierce Arrow Sales Corporation, with facilities throughout the country. Car sales thereafter would be through private distributors. This further hurt sales. Between August 1934 and May 1935 all of these Pierce-Arrow sales facilities were sold. While in receivership the federal court in Buffalo was regulating the number of cars that could be produced. This limitation prevented the sale of cars for which there were orders.

The number of factory employees, relatively stable before, was reduced to about 800. The reorganized company became the Pierce-Arrow Motor Corporation and was operating free of bankruptcy by May 1935.

1935
Models 845, 1245, and 1255
During those turbulent times not much effort was directed toward altering the design of the models. Consequently the three models of 1935 introduced in January were essentially unchanged from 1934. A differentiating feature was the three hood doors, now arranged in a straight line with a chrome rib. Also, the headlight lenses were much more convex. They were designated: Model 845 (a 140-horsepower

straight eight on a 139-inch or 144-inch chassis), Model 1245 (a V-12 with 175-horsepower on a 139-inch or 144-inch chassis), and the Model 1255 (which was the custom V-12 on the 147-inch chassis). Style variations were cut down to nine including the Production Silver Arrow. Pierce still offered custom-bodied cars by Brunn. A new style dashboard and instrument panel was used. There were two large dials on either side of the steering column containing the instruments.

The federal government must have kept its faith in the Pierce-Arrow Company and its car, for in the spring of 1935 it took delivery of two blue limousines, with bulletproof glass and armor plate for J. Edgar Hoover (car number 3540021 still exists). With all of its troubles, Pierce only made 875 cars that year. The loss of a sales organization was a major cause in the sales drop. During mid-1935 the company introduced nine and fifteen-passenger commercial vehicles (see Chapter 9). These low-production items were again a desperation measure designed to stimulate sales. The effort did no good, and losses continued, totalling about $200,000 for the year. The company reorganized slightly, and an attempt was made to generate some cash by a new stock issue, but it was of no significant help.

1936
Models 1601, 1602, and 1603
In November 1935 Pierce brought out the new line for 1936. The design had undergone a major change, although the generally rounded body styles appeared similar to those of 1935. A total of twelve styles were available, including a very beautiful Custom Brunn Metropolitan Town Brougham. Prices ranged from about $4,000 to $7,300. This was the last optimistic effort to remain viable, and the company went for broke.

Again there were the three standard chassis: Model 1601 with the 150-horsepower, eight-cylinder engine on a 139-inch wheelbase (four body styles); Model 1602 with the 185-horsepower V-12 engine on a 139-inch or 144-inch-wheelbase chassis (six body styles); and the Model 1603, which was the same as the 1602 except for the 147-inch wheelbase (two body styles). Actually, the Model 1601 could be ordered with a 144-inch or a 147-inch wheelbase and in other body styles.

Mechanically, the car was an example of excellent engineering. These cars, made during the final period of business failure, represent some of the finest of Pierce-Arrows. Unfortunately, the company did not read the times or the public taste correctly. It was not fashionable to be rich, and certainly not to be ostentatious. Still, Pierce advertising talked about the "Pierce-Arrow type of owner." They should have taken a lesson from Marie Antoinette.

The body styles were rounded considerably, a design in vogue as the classical period declined, but not very attractive by today's collectors' tastes. A top-hinged trunk was integral with the body on all models except those with a rumble seat. The front view was unique, with "quad" lights and a very flat radiator grill. The "quad" lights offered five lighting variations controlled by a dash switch and a foot switch indicated by red and green dash lights. These were parking lights, bright beam, long range, country driving light, city driving down-beam, and cross-beam passing light. The new dashboard had two large dials on either side of the steering column. A permanently-mounted archer was fixed on the pointed radiator shell. The standard 17-inch wheel was a steel artillery type, but a very stylish optional chrome wheel disk cover was available, over wire wheels.

The box girder frame was reinforced with an "X" member. The engine was moved forward and the steering box was placed in an awkward position in front of the front axle. This caused the steering column to approach the driver at a rather flat, and poorly-accepted, angle from its place in the dashboard between the large dials. After the first seventy-five cars were made this way, the steering column angle was changed back to the more conventional inclination, with the steering column beneath the dash. This necessitated two universal joints coupling the column with the steering box.

Another of the thirty-six major mechanical changes touted by Pierce advertising was the incorporation of an overdrive unit directly behind the gear box, bolted to the rear of the transmission case. This Warner R-1 unit was coupled by a spline to the main shaft. It contained a planetary gear arrangement activated by a centrifugal clutch. The rear end ratio was changed to 4.58 to 1. With the overdrive engaged, the effective rear ratio was changed to 3.23 to 1. Speeds up to 90 miles per hour could be comfortably

obtained! Since the overdrive unit was located where the power brake system had been on previous models, the company went to a Bendix vacuum booster brake which could exert 290-power pull on the brake shoe. The vacuum brake was similar to that used on the Series 36 ten years earlier. The freewheeling unit was built into the overdrive case as well.

Raising the compression ratio of 6.4 to 1 increased the horsepower to 150 and 185 for the eight and V-12 engines respectively. A new muffler system employed four units in series suspended by rubber mounts. The four different units were tuned to eliminate noise, but creating practically no back pressure. Hydraulic valve lifters were again used. The interiors were of beautiful Laidlow cloth, and Kapoc was used to insulate for temperature and sound.

From the standpoint of engineering design and workmanship, the 1936 car was a beautiful machine. Pierce was still trying to make the best car possible, but times had changed, and there was little demand for this type of car.

Lincoln, Cadillac, and Packard were bringing out moderately-priced cars which they were able to sell during the Depression. Although the 1936 Pierce-Arrow looked less classical in style than in previous years, it represented one of the finest cars Pierce ever made.

The company had been advertising heavily in newspapers and magazines during 1934-36. But in 1936 the emphasis switched to direct mailing of material to the homes of those able to afford a Pierce-Arrow. Despite these efforts, sales for 1936 dropped to 787 units.

Meanwhile, in August 1936, the company announced its entrance into the newly-popular trailer manufacturing field (see chapter 9). Apparently, this effort had little positive effect on the company's finances.

1937
Models 1701, 1702 and 1703

The company announced the 1937 models in October 1936. These cars (Models 1701, 1702, and 1703) were externally the same as the 1936 cars. In fact, most factory advertising for 1937 used the photographs from 1936 with some retouching. The only recognizable difference was in the interior design, mainly on the dashboard. In late 1936 and early 1937 automobile production dropped sharply, presumably to emphasize Travelodge production. New cars were primarily used for publicity purposes. Car production for 1937 was only 167 units. Some Pierce-Arrow historians put the number at 177 units. At any rate, the number was quite small. The company was all but dead. The only two new models were an Enclosed-Driver Opera Limousine and a 144-inch W.B. Five-Passenger Sedan. Very few were built, and only one of each is thought to survive.

In a last-minute effort to hold on, a reorganization was planned. The plan announced August 6, 1937, was to raise $10.7 million by the sale of 1.3 million shares of stock and to build a medium-priced automobile along with the traditional Pierce-Arrow and the Travelodge. President Arthur Chanter proposed three alternative production possibilities:

Pierce-Arrow Units	Medium-Priced Cars Units	Trailers Units	Earnings
A) 1,200	25,000	4,800	$1,800,000
B) 1,200	35,000	4,800	$3,100,000
C) 2,400	45,000	10,000	$5,750,000

In order to give impetus to the reorganization plan, it was rumored that an "important person," Postmaster General James Farley or Boston banker George Sweet, would become chairman of the board of Pierce-Arrow. On September 2, 1937, the stockholders approved the plan to reorganize.

Due to a depression in the stock market and a business recession in 1937, the stock issue was delayed and then scrapped. Postmaster General Farley did not join Pierce-Arrow. An interim bank loan was obtained, however, of $52,000 (losses from July 1936 through November 1937 had been $224,000).

1938
Models 1801, 1802, and 1803
The 1938 models were announced in October 1937. These were identical to the 1937 models except for a banjo-type steering wheel made by Sheller, and a repositioned hand brake hung under the dashboard. Also, the illuminated license plate frame was moved from the left rear fender to the center of the trunk on some closed models.

It is uncertain how many 1938 model cars were made. Some sources say only seventeen. Certainly there were very few. The Pierce-Arrow Society lists ten as surviving. The cars were hand-fabricated from 1937 parts beginning in October 1937 as the orders trickled in. For all practical purposes, real manufacturing ceased in mid-1937. The still hopeful company reserved a spot in the 1938 New York show, but no 1938 promotional material was ever made. The 1938 models were exhibited at very few auto shows.

In December 1937 the company petitioned to reorganize under Section 77B of the Bankruptcy Act, as another temporizing measure. Judge John Knight approved the petition, and after the first hearing on January 17, 1938, the matter was still a stalemate. Federal Judge J. R. Hazel and Martin Ewald, secretary-treasurer of Pierce-Arrow, were appointed as custodial cotrustees. At the second hearing, March 10, 1938, William Morey, attorney for the trustees of the company, said that they would soon be able to decide the fate of the company. At this point, Pierce-Arrow had 444 creditors, and a sale of part of the physical assets was sought.

Judge Knight ordered an auction of $200,000 worth of tools on March 22 (at the insistence of Walter E. Schott of Cincinnati, who was owed $200,000). The trustees requested a hearing of the stockholders and creditors to decide whether to liquidate. This was set for April 11, but on March 28, Judge Knight ruled the corporation insolvent and ordered liquidation of the assets. It was estimated that there was book value of assets totaling $2,768,822, an actual realizable value of $1,197,771, and liabilities of $1,892,745. The only creditors to receive any money were the Marine Trust Company of Buffalo, the New York Federal Reserve Bank, and Walter Schott of Cincinnati.

The trustees were authorized to exhibit and sell the factory assets. A newly-formed group, the 1685 Elmwood Avenue Corporation, bought the plant for $40,000 and acceptance of $1,350,000 in back debts. It would continue to provide service and parts until 1942. After that, parts were scrapped for the war effort (a pity). The Morey Machine Company was placed in charge of listing and selling all the contents of the building. Throughout 1938, the tools and sundries were sold piecemeal from the factory. The marked-down prices made the great quiet building look like a wholesale house.

Although the Pierce-Arrow Motor Corporation

ceased to function in March 1938, the company was not legally dissolved by the secretary of the state of New York until December 14, 1944. One story has it that the last car to leave the factory in the early summer of 1938 was a hand-fabricated twelve-cylinder sedan built by Engineer Don Anson and a couple of fellow workers for Chief Engineer Karl Wise. The individual parts had been purchased from the receivers. Karl Wise went on to become the chief engineer at Bendix Aviation Corporation. Supposedly, in 1941 a "bastardized" Pierce was assembled from different parts (mostly 1934) for a Mr. Robbins.

Epilogue

Much reminiscing has taken place about Pierce-Arrow's demise. Where did it go wrong? Prominent before World War I, the company's self-satisfaction kept it from progressing in the 1920s. Once behind, it was never able to catch up. Sales success in the early 1930s lulled it into false security. Studebaker was covering its losses, until not even Studebaker could withstand the financial overextension. Production of a moderately priced car much earlier might have kept it

solvent, but with temporarily good sales Pierce did not feel the need for the lower-priced model. Besides, this would have put it into direct competition with Studebaker. Pierce-Arrow certainly made one of the highest-quality cars of the mid-1930s, but depressive and numerous "bad breaks" forced it under.

It is interesting to contemplate what might have happened if it had been able to survive until some World War II contracts could again swell its profits, as happened in World War I. Perhaps it would have succumbed anyway in the postwar race, along with Packard, Hudson and Studebaker.

It is difficult to imagine a "Pierce-Arrow" in the present-day genre—a Pierce with plastic dashboard, rubber bumpers, synthetic fabrics, and an engine stifled by government pollution controls. Perhaps it is well that the company died when it did—in the autumn of the "classic" period. The memory of Pierce-Arrow has not been tarnished by the production of any automobile that was not "the very finest that could be made." Today the name of Pierce-Arrow calls to mind the elegant motoring of an Edwardian period that may never again return.

The 1933 Silver Arrow. The spare wheel was concealed in the front fender. Only five of these show cars were made ($10,000 each). Four have survived. (Courtesy of the Motor Vehicle Manufacturers Association.)

The 1933 Silver Arrow incorporated many new ideas. (Courtesy of the University of Michigan.)

The standard cars in 1933 were slightly more streamlined than those of 1932, and were quite attractive. The headlights had a curve continuous with the line of the fender. This reversed curvature was reminiscent of the shape that first appeared in 1914.

Custom Salon Club Brougham...Model 1242...by Pierce-Arrow

The 1933 Model 1242 Tourer and Club Brougham with V-12 engine and 142-inch wheelbase. (Courtesy of the University of Michigan.)

Custom Salon Seven Passenger Sedan...Model 1242...by Pierce Arrow

Custom Salon Club Sedan...Model 1247...by Pierce Arrow

(This Model also is built as a Club Berline with Driver's Compartment Partition)

The 1933 Model 1242 seven-passenger Sedan and Club Sedan. The headlights had a new curvature reminiscent of the 1914 Series 2 cars. (Courtesy of the University of Michigan.)

The 1933 LeBaron Convertible Victoria and Convertible Sedan (Model 1247). Two of the most "classic" Pierce-Arrows ever made. (Courtesy of the University of Michigan.)

Le Baron Seven Passenger Enclosed Drive Limousine . . . Model 1247

A 1933 LeBaron Enclosed-Driver Limousine and 1933 LeBaron Club Sedan (note "V" windshield).
(Courtesy of the University of Michigan.)

Because of good sales in the early 1930s, world speed records, industry firsts, and the revolutionary Silver-Arrow, perhaps there was some cause for optimism in 1933. Even though Studebaker went into receivership in April of that year, the Pierce management felt a renewed hope and enthusiasm in its reorganization.

The stylish dashboard a 1933 LeBaron Pierce-Arrow.

The all-new 1934 Coupe and Club Brougham. The radiator shell had less chrome and the archer was permanently fixed on the radiator shell. (Courtesy of the University of Michigan.)

The 1934 Enclosed-Driver Limousine and the five-passenger Sedan. The styles were losing the "classic look." (Courtesy of the Motor Vehicle Manufacturers Association.)

Top—The 1934 "production" Silver Arrow. It had lost the beautiful look of the 1933 Silver Arrow. Few of these were made. (Courtesy of the University of Michigan.) *Bottom*—The 1934 Town Car by Brunn. (Courtesy of the University of Michigan.)

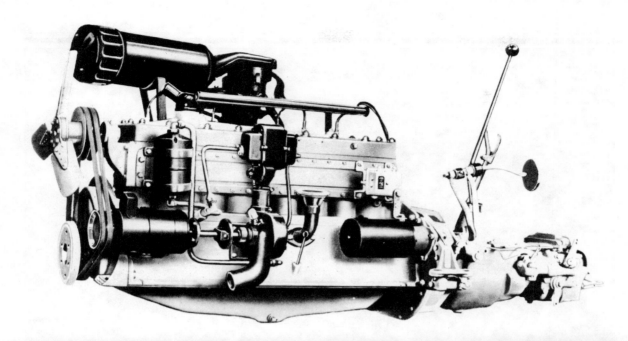

Top—The 1934 eight-cylinder engine. It developed 140 horsepower at 3,400 rpm. Note the "Startex" above the starter motor. (Courtesy of the Motor Vehicle Manufacturers Association.) *Bottom*—The stock certificate of the reorganized Pierce-Arrow Motor Car Company (1934). (Courtesy of the Pierce-Arrow Society.)

The 1935 Convertible Coupe Roadster and Coupe. The hood ventilating doors were different from those on the 1934 models. (Courtesy of the Pierce-Arrow Society.)

The 1935 Silver Arrow and Club Sedan (with blind rear quarter). Note the disc wheel covers.
(Courtesy of the Pierce-Arrow Society.)

The 1935 Sedan and Enclosed-Driver Limousine. (Courtesy of the Pierce-Arrow Society.)

The 1936 Convertible Coupe and Coupe. This was the last year of new body styles. The grill was again less impressive. (Courtesy of the University of Michigan.)

The 1936 Club Sedan and five-passenger Sedan. The engineering was superior, but the styles were uninspired. (Courtesy of the University of Michigan.)

Top—The 1936 Enclosed-Driver Limousine. (Courtesy of the University of Michigan.) *Bottom*—The 1937 custom Brunn Metropolitan Town Brougham. This was one of the prettiest of the last models. (Courtesy of the Motor Vehicle Manufacturers Association.)

Top—The 1936 front end showing the quad lights, used in 1936, 1937, and 1938. (Courtesy of the Motor Vehicle Manufacturers Association.) *Bottom*—The 1937 Model 1702 Convertible Sedan. (Courtesy of the Motor Vehicle Manufacturers Association.)

An Invitation to Discontent
... with all others

● **Step in and start.** The silken power of 185 thoroughbreds is yours to command. One mile—and discontent with all other cars begins.

Drive . . . over hills and on the roughest roads, maneuver through the crowded traffic lanes of city streets . . . and learn discontent with any performance that falls short of new Pierce-Arrow standards now revealed.

Stop . . . in full flight. Effortless braking brings the car to a velvet-smooth stop in less than half the distance safety laws demand. Two and three-tenths seconds to stop at forty miles an hour. Twenty-two stringent state laws allow six seconds.

Compare, point by point, with any other car. You will find Pierce-Arrow unequaled in power, in silence, smoothness, stability and safety. Compare the sheer luxury of its appointments. Compare your own degree of relaxation at the wheel . . . your confidence, the delight and justified pride that are yours when you drive this car.

If you are one of those who must know WHY these things are true, compare every mechanical specification. Put the car on a rack and look at it from beneath . . . or come to Pierce-Arrow's great factory and see it built with all of today's most modern precision equipment by master craftsmen who, for thirty-six years, have been building fine cars exclusively.

The innate luxury, the matchless comfort, the breath-taking beauty, the superb performance, and, perhaps above all, *the greater safety* of this car of cars yield priceless dividends in satisfaction and pride in the ownership of what is recognized everywhere as America's finest motor car.

This is an invitation to discontent with all other motor cars, because it is an invitation to test the new Pierce-Arrow *in your own way*. Accept it, if you will, in this spirit . . . as a friendly challenge to that eternal discontent that step by step leads you to the finest in everything.

PIERCE-ARROW MOTOR CORPORATION, BUFFALO, N. Y.

Pierce-Arrow's new six per cent payment plan offers a sound, convenient method of paying out of income.

PIERCE-ARROW

THE ONE GREAT NAME THAT IDENTIFIES
FINE CARS EXCLUSIVELY

The final uninspired promotional efforts from Pierce-Arrow (1936). Note the dash's two large instrument dials.
(Courtesy of the Pierce-Arrow Society)

Truck Models
R-E and R-F

Pierce
Arrow
HEAVY DUTY
MOTOR TRUCKS

9

TRUCKS, BUSES, AND TRAVELODGES

The First Truck

Although Pierce-Arrow was primarily in the automobile manufacturing business, it did make commercial vehicles sporadically during its existence. The Great Arrow had been developed by 1905 and was found to be a well-running, reliable car. That same year the Pierce directors decided to design and produce a Pierce truck. Fergusson and May went to Europe to study European-built trucks (which, like European cars, were more advanced than our vehicles). They settled on a five-ton capacity with chain drive as the optimum design. A cab-over-engine design was used to shorten the truck. Modified parts were borrowed from the 45-horsepower touring car. The clutch was the cone type and was connected with a three-forward-and-reverse gearbox. The bevel-gear jack shaft axle then drove both rear wheels by means of bilateral roller chains (Timken bearings were specified).

Work on the truck was delayed by the company's move into the new Elmwood Avenue plant in November 1906. A prototype was completed in March 1907 and, after testing, went into service for the Goodrich Rubber Company in Akron, Ohio. Testing and evaluation of this truck continued while it was in use.

By 1909, the directors decided to build 100 models of this first truck. In September of that year, H. Kerr

Thomas arrived as assistant general manager. He had been with the Napier Company of England, and before that, with the Hallford Company of England that made the "Saurer" (Swiss-designed) truck. From his trucking experience, he suggested to May changes that he felt would improve the quality of the Pierce truck. As a result the one hundred scheduled trucks were not built, and on April 30, 1910, Thomas started to design a new five-ton truck. This had a roller-chain drive with the driver seated behind the engine. When the design was completed, plans were made to produce 200 trucks.

In May 1910, May and Fergusson met a Canadian who was so enthusiastic about the gear-driven trucks used by his company that, after visiting Toronto, they again stopped work on the truck design. After considerable debate, they decided to adopt a worm-gear drive, which they thought would be more serviceable than bevel-and-spur-gear or chain drive. This new truck design was roughly modeled after a 2½-ton Leland worm-drive truck that Fergusson had seen in England two years earlier.

Thomas quickly redesigned the Pierce five-ton truck to incorporate the overslung worm-gear drive. The gears were ordered from David Brown and Company of England. At that time all American trucks were using chain drive, which did not give lengthy or quiet service. With Pierce's introduction of worm-gear-driven trucks on December 24, 1910, a quality truck became available in the United States. Its reputation for high-performance brought high sales. The truck was exhibited at the New York show in January 1911. The first truck sold went to the International Brewing Corporation on June 2, 1911. So in 1911, after six years of planning, Pierce had a line of high-quality five-ton trucks. The truck division was directed by H. K. Thomas and John Younger. The early models, were tested by Frances W. Davis, a young Harvard graduate, who had joined Pierce-Arrow in 1910. His experience in testing the early hard-to-steer trucks led him to invent power steering in 1926, which he first installed on his 1921 Series 32 roadster—Serial No. 322426, Engine No. 322441. Even though he put the power steering on his Pierce-Arrow it was after he had left the company. Throughout his life he tried to regain this Series 32 car, but to date its whereabouts are unknown. The power steering unit itself is in the Smithsonian Institution. From his experience in World War I, Davis also devised and patented (in 1921) a slip differential, but it was never utilized by the company. When Younger retired in 1918 as chief truck engineer, Davis succeeded him. Because of turmoil and the lack of progressive policies at Pierce, Davis left the company in 1922 to become a private consulting engineer. He died April 16, 1978.

That first Pierce truck was a five-ton stake-bed design with hard-rubber tires. It was designated as Model X-1. Soon an open top was available. The truck was equipped with side lamps but no headlights. The engine was four-cylinders, cast in pairs (at this time the automobiles had only six-cylinder engines, with three different horsepower ratings available). The bore and stroke on the "T" head truck engines were 4⅞ inches x 6 inches, giving a horsepower of 38 (A.L.A.M. rating). The transmission had three forward gears and one reverse gear. The front tire was 36 inches x 5 inches, while the rear was 40 inches x 6 inches. The wheelbase was 156 inches. The cost for the chassis was $4,500. This advanced Pierce design set a new standard in the United States.

Characteristic of this first design, used in 1911 and 1912, were the hood without louvers and the radiator with horizontal louvers.

In October 1913 a two-ton truck, Model X-2, was added to the line. Its similar but smaller engine had a

4 inch x 5½ inch bore and stroke, producing 25.6 horsepower. Two wheelbases were available, 150 inches and 180 inches. The models of 1913 can be distinguished by the four louvers on the side of the hood, four openings in the side of the radiator shell, and vertical elements in the radiator front.

Exact truck production figures are not available, but as World War I approached, automobile production at Pierce-Arrow was relatively de-emphasized while truck production grew rapidly. Several foreign contracts, notably English and French, stimulated this growth. By 1917 the annual truck output was over 7,000 units, while that of automobiles was only 2,500. This emphasis on truck production was a factor in Pierce-Arrow's falling behind in automobile design after the war. Many thousands of Pierce-Arrow trucks saw service in Europe during World War I. By 1918 Pierce had produced 14,000 trucks. After the war, used Pierce trucks were plentiful in England at very reasonable prices. Ironically, very few trucks have survived, although one was around in England after World War II.

In 1915 the five-ton and two-ton trucks were designated as R-5 and X-2 respectively, but they were little changed over a period of several years, from 1913 until 1920. A 1918 Pierce specification sheet lists the two-ton truck (X-4) at $3,750 and the five-ton model (R-9) at $5,500. During this long period modifications occurred, but the basic chassis changed little. As a result, sales of the prestigious truck dropped to 709 in 1921, although the recession of 1921 was undoubtedly a factor. Interestingly, Packard dropped its truck line in 1922.

A 3½ ton model W-2 truck was added to the line in 1920-21. This contained a four-cylinder (4½ inch x 6¾ inch) engine producing 32 horsepower. The price was $4,950. Production of the R-10, X-5, and W-2 trucks ceased in 1922, and new models were introduced.

In 1923 the truck line underwent a major change. Several ranges of load capacity were available. In addition, a four-cylinder dual-valve engine was introduced in the trucks. The specifications for these models are shown in the table at the top of page 205.

These same model chassis also were available in tractors and tractor dump trucks. Despite this expanded new line, sales did not do well, with less than 2,000 being produced per year. General auto sales at

Model	Bore & Stroke	HP	Capacity	Price
X-A	4 x 5½	25	2–2½ tons	—
X-B	4 x 5½	25	2½–3 tons	—
W-C	4½ x 6¾	32	2–4 tons	—
W-D	4½ x 6¾	32	4–5 tons	—
R-E	4½ x 6¾	32	5–6 tons	$5,100
R-F	4½ x 6¾	32	6–7½ tons	$5,400

Pierce were also declining at this time, with profits following. Money needed to revitalize the truck line was spent trying to save the automobile market (by bringing out the Series 80 model in 1924). Without forward-thinking leadership in the truck division, Pierce's share of the market continued to slip.

Model Z Chassis

The year 1924 saw the introduction of a new Z chassis that utilized the six-cylinder dual-valve engine of the Series 33 automobile. This had a 4 inch x 5½ inch bore and stroke and developed 38 horsepower. It came in two wheelbases, 196-inch and 220-inch. With its four-speed transmission, it had a top speed of 60 miles per hour. The price was between $3,300 and $5,200. Although primarily made for a bus body, this chassis was also used for other commercial vehicles, including a number of fire engines. Scanty information from Pierce-Arrow recension tables would indicate that rather few (less than a thousand) Z chassis were assembled between 1924 and 1928. Two presently are known to exist.

Fleet Arrow (1928)

During this period of financial crisis, another truck chassis was brought out in hopes of stimulating truck sales. This was the Fleet Arrow panel truck (Model FA) of 1928. The stake body and other styles were made. The 70-horsepower, six-cylinder "L"-head engine was basically a reworked Series 80 engine with 3½ inch x 5 inch bore and stroke. Wheelbases available were 140-inch, 160-inch, and 180-inch. Slightly over 500 of these trucks were made before truck production was completely halted in May 1929 to reassess the company's truck position. By this time Studebaker had merged with Pierce-Arrow; the break in truck production was to allow the company to redesign the truck line.

In December 1930 the new truck line was introduced and consisted of the models PT (70-horsepower, 2-ton), PW (77-horsepower, 3-ton), PX (103-horsepower, 4-ton), PY (103-horsepower, 5-ton), and PZ (130-horsepower, 8-ton). These five models all utilized a new six-cylinder engine (the car line at this time used only the new straight eight). Encouraged by the increased auto sales and profits of 1930, Pierce came out with a bigger line of trucks. No records exist to indicate just how many trucks were actually produced during 1931 and 1932, but the figure is probably fewer than 200. By November, 1932 all truck production was stopped at Pierce-Arrow. Studebaker had acquired the White Motor Corporation of Cleveland, a financial overextension as it turned out. Trucks carrying the Pierce-Arrow name were manufactured by White at Cleveland in 1932 and 1933. The trucks were listed as "available" as late as 1935.

White Motor "Pierce-Arrow" Trucks

The many models made by the White Motor Corporation had unusual designations:

13S385	22R479	27T361T
15T298	22X479	34T361T
17T361	22X479	35R479T
18W361	24X479	45X479T
19R479	28Y479	60M611T
21W361	28M611	75M779T
	34K611	

The first two numbers indicated the maximum gross weight rating in thousands of pounds, while the last three numbers indicated the engine's cubic-inch displacement.

The White Motor Corporation ceased making trucks in 1935, but the Seagrave Corporation of Columbus, Ohio, producers of fine fire engines, bought the rights to produce V-12 and eight-cylinder Pierce-Arrow engines. They also purchased the tooling. Thus Pierce-Arrow designed engines lived on in the Seagrave fire engines.

According to fire-truck historian John Gambs, the last Seagrave fire engine with a Pierce-Arrow type V-12 engine was delivered in 1970. Many Pierce-powered rigs remain in front-line service throughout the country today. The fact that Seagrave did little but add dual-ignition attests to the superb engineering of the V-12, especially when one considers the demands put upon fire engine power plants.

A curious finding is apparent in examining one of these Seagrave engines. The word "Seagrave" is cast in large letters on each head. But also cast into the head is a small hexagon containing the two letters "P-A"! That magic name lives on.

After the cessation of truck production, Pierce built a few small nine and fifteen-passenger buses in 1935. The eight-cylinder 140-horsepower chassis was stretched to a 204-inch wheelbase. Actually, it was just an airport limousine type of car.

Travelodge

Pierce-Arrow automobile sales did well in the early 1930s, but dwindled as the Depression worsened. As in the 1920s, lack of money had become a severe problem, and all measures were considered to try to remain solvent. One of the last-ditch efforts at Pierce was its entrance into the travel-trailer field, first among the car manufacturers, although travel trailers were already becoming popular with the motoring public.

In August 1936, Pierce-Arrow formally announced its intention to produce the Travelodge, which came in three models: a 19-foot Model A; a 16½-foot Model B; and a 13½-foot Model C. The prices for the fully-equipped models were $1,282, $972 and $784, respectively. A separate division within the company was set up to produce the trailers. As with its automobile, Pierce made the finest quality Travelodge that it knew how. Unfortunately, the efforts were in vain this late in the decline of the company. The first Travelodges were made in September 1936 (classed as a 1937 model), and production probably continued until early 1937. Estimates put the total production at about 450 units (105 Model A; 261 Model B; and 74 Model C). The Pierce-Arrow Society lists at least thirteen survivors.

The design called for a steel frame with an 18-gauge sheet aluminum body. The interior was lined with plywood of birch and gum. Electrolytic action at the riveted aluminum skin and the steel frame caused considerable corrosion.

Although it was not required by law then, Pierce-Arrow equipped the trailer with a Bendix hydraulic brake actuated from a vacuum cylinder, which was connected by a hose to the trailering car. The independent wheel suspension was designed to require no lubrication. The trunions were rubber-mounted for a quieter ride.

The interiors were equipped with a refrigerator (i.e., ice box), water tank, dinette (with seats opening to a double bed), gasoline cooking stove, wood-burning stove, and lavatory. These provided the traveler with all of the comforts, in case anyone in the Depression had enough money to vacation. This facet of the Pierce-Arrow history was, unfortunately, quite brief. By 1937 the company was unsuccessfully struggling to keep production going. It advertised the Travelodge during 1937, but with little response. Thus, the last of the Pierce-Arrow commercial vehicles joined the pages of history.

Enter the collector.

The first experimental five-ton truck (circa 1906) with chain drive. The cab-over-engine configuration was not retained. (Courtesy of the Motor Vehicle Manufacturers Association.)

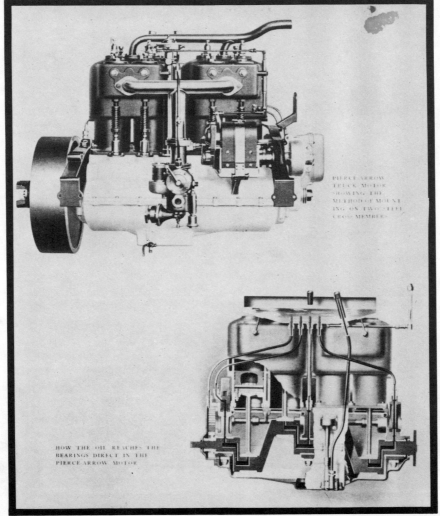

Top—The first production five-ton truck, introduced in 1911. The radiator had horizontal louvers, but the hood had none. (Courtesy of the University of Michigan.) *Bottom*—The 1911 truck engine was a redesigned 45-horsepower, four-cylinder car engine. (Courtesy of the Motor Vehicle Manufacturers Association.)

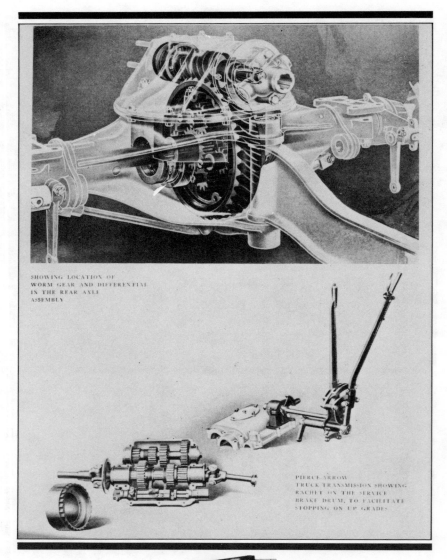

SHOWING LOCATION OF
WORM GEAR AND DIFFERENTIAL
IN THE REAR AXLE
ASSEMBLY

PIERCE ARROW
TRUCK TRANSMISSION SHOWING
RACHET ON THE SERVICE
BRAKE DRUM, TO FACILITATE
STOPPING ON UP GRADES

Top—The 1911 worm-gear drive and transmission. In using the worm gear, Pierce-Arrow set a standard for the industry. (Courtesy of the Motor Vehicle Manufacturers Association.) *Bottom*—Francis Davis in his 1921 Pierce-Arrow Roadster, which utilized the power-steering unit that he invented in 1926. (Courtesy of the Pierce-Arrow Society.)

Top—The power-steering unit is now in the Smithsonian Institution. The whereabouts of the Roadster is unknown (engine #322441). (Courtesy of the Pierce-Arrow Society.) *Bottom*—The first model five-ton truck of 1911 with solid rubber tires. (Courtesy of the University of Michigan.)

The first Pierce truck was a five-ton stake-bed design with hard-rubber tires. It was designated as Model X-1. Soon an open top was available. The truck was equipped with side lamps but no headlights.

Top—The two-ton truck introduced in October 1913. The radiator and hood louvers were different. (Courtesy of the University of Michigan.) *Bottom*—A bus made on a Pierce-Arrow chassis (circa 1913). Note the gas headlights. (Courtesy of the University of Michigan.)

Top—A fire truck on a Series 3 car chassis (circa 1915). Engine House #36 in Buffalo, New York, was built in 1913. (Courtesy of the University of Michigan.) *Center and bottom*—The X-2 (two-ton) truck with different applications. (Courtesy of the Pierce-Arrow Society.)

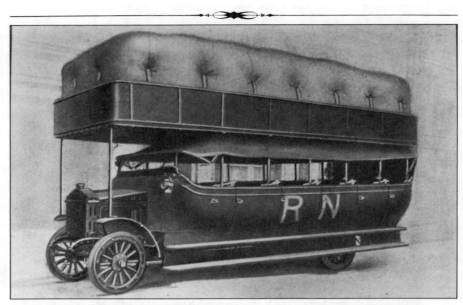

Truck Models
R-E and R-F

Top—An X-2 used in England. Due to the fuel shortage, this was converted to operate on "coal gas." (Courtesy of the Pierce-Arrow Society.) *Bottom*—An advertisement for R-E and R-F trucks, made between 1923 and 1927. Very few trucks of this period have survived. (Courtesy of the Pierce-Arrow Society.)

Top—This body, built by the Knightstown Buggy Company on a truck chassis, was delivered to the Notre Dame Academy in Cincinnati, Ohio, in November 1920. (Courtesy of the University of Michigan.) *Bottom*—The North Greece fire truck circa 1920. (What state?) (Courtesy of the University of Michigan.)

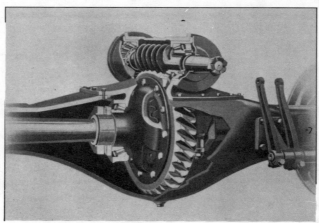

Top—A 1928 Fleet Arrow truck. (Courtesy of the University of Michigan.) *Bottom*—The interior of the worm drive of a 1921 two-ton truck. (Courtesy of the University of Michigan.)

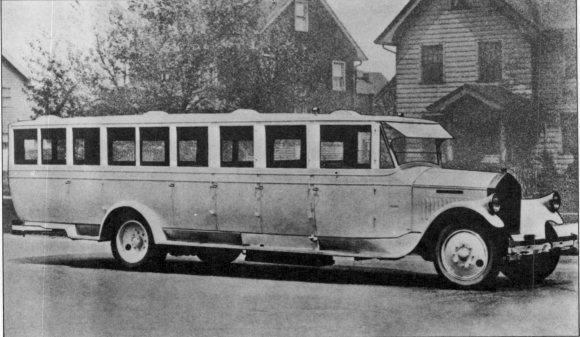

The Z chassis (1924–1928) was used for fire trucks and buses. (Courtesy of the Pierce-Arrow Society.)

Top—The Z chassis was also used for coaches and mobile homes. (Courtesy of the Pierce-Arrow Society.)
Bottom—This circa 1935 funeral car carries a Henney body. (Courtesy of the Pierce-Arrow Society.)

The 13 S 385 Pierce-Arrow Truck Chassis

Maximum Gross Weight Rating—13,000 lbs. (chassis, cab, body and payload).

Nominal rating—2 to 2 1/2 tons—for licensing purposes.

Standard Wheelbases	***Chassis Weight*** Front	Rear	Total	Turning Radius
160"	3,000 lbs.	2,750 lbs.	5,750 lbs.	24'
180"	3,020 lbs.	2,780 lbs.	5,800 lbs.	27'
200"	3,040 lbs.	2,810 lbs.	5,850 lbs.	31' 6"

Weights include gas, water and oil, but no cab.

Chassis Dimensions (in inches).

Wheelbase	160	180	200*
Overall Length	232	252	272
Back of cab to C/L of rear axle	62 9/16	82 9/16	102 9/16
Back of cab to end of frame	116 5/8	136 5/8	156 5/8
Back of dash to C/L of rear axle	115 13/16	135 13/16	155 13/16
Back of dash to end of frame	169 7/8	189 7/8	209 7/8
Tread—with standard tires	Front—65"	Rear—67 7/16"	
Road Clearance with 8.25/20 tires	Front—10 1/4"	Rear—9 3/4"	
Height—Ground to top of frame loaded	Front—25 1/8"	Rear—28 29/32"	
Frame width	34"		

Rear Axle Ratios Available	***Rear Tire Equipment*** Size	Type	***Engine Speed***	***Road Speed***
5 2/7	8.25/20	Balloons	2,800	55 M.P.H.
5 2/7	34 x 7	High Pressure	2,800	55 M.P.H.
6 1/6	8.25/20	Balloons	2,800	47 M.P.H.
6 1/6	34 x 7	High Pressure	2,800	47 M.P.H.

Engine: Eight cylinder—3 1/2" bore—5" stroke—Displacement 385 cu. in. N.A.C.C. horsepower rating 39.2—Actual horsepower—125 at 2,800 R.P.M. (Governed engine speed.) Maximum torque 274 ft. pounds at 1,000 R.P.M. Engine and transmission combined in one unit. Engine supported on rugged frame brackets mounted on rubber four point suspension. Nine bearing statically and dynamically balanced drop forged steel crankshaft—2 3/8" dia. Total main bearing length 14 1/8". Lanchester variable type balancer back of No. 1 main bearing insures smooth running. Connecting rods of drop forged steel—have centrifugally cast bearings 1 3/4" long x 2 1/4" in dia. Detachable cylinder head of "L" type. Inlet valves 1 1/2" clear diameter—exhaust valves 1 3/8" clear diameter.

Lubrication: Engine—pressure feed from gear type oil pump driven by camshaft direct to main, connecting rod, camshaft bearings and timing chain. Removable oil filter easily accessible for replacement. Chassis—high pressure grease connections.

Cooling System: Radiator—of flat tube and fin construction—flexibly supported on frame side rails—Capacity—6 3/4 gallons—centrifugal water pump and six blade fan driven from crankshaft pulley by two Vee type fan belts.

Ignition: Battery type semi-automatic distributor direct gear drive from camshaft—coil mounted on dash.

Generator: Six volt third brush, thermostatically regulated type—driven by dual Vee type fan belts.

Battery: 19 plate 6 volt rubber separator type—160 ampere hour capacity—mounted in metal box rubber cushioned.

Starting Motor: 6 volt dual reduction outboard bearing type with steel ring gear on flywheel.

Carburetor: Duplex design with two mixing chambers—spring actuated choke to prevent overpriming. Fitted with copper mesh air cleaner and carburetor silencer—automatic thermostatically controlled manifold heater.

Fuel System: Camshaft driven fuel pump mounted on engine—25 gallon gasoline tank mounted under driver's seat. Gas tank straps—spring equipped to eliminate strain due to weaving.

Governor: Velocity type fully sealed to prevent tampering.

Controls: Clutch, service brake, accelerator pedal and starter switch plunger on toe boards. Gear shift and hand brake lever at center. Horn button and spark and throttle hand controls on steering column. Ammeter, ignition and lighting switch, lock, speedometer, oil gauge, gas gauge, engine temperature indicator and choke mounted on instrument board.

Clutch: Two plate dry disc clutch fully adjustable with fully enclosed pilot ball-bearing in flywheel. Clutch throwout bearing of ball thrust type. Clutch is entirely enclosed and readily accessible.

Transmission: Four speed selective type—unit mounted. All gears and shafts are alloy steel. Shift lever mounted directly above gear box. Provision for power take-off on both sides with Std. S.A.E. large opening.

Standard Gear Ratios:

First	6.18 to 1
Second	3.20 to 1
Third	1.90 to 1
High	1 to 1
Reverse	8.65 to 1

Propeller Shafts and Universal Joints: Tubular drive shaft with three all metal, fully enclosed universal joints and self-aligning intermediate bearing transmits power from transmission to rear axle.

Rear Axle: Full floating—Spiral Bevel type—alloy steel axle shafts carrying driving torque only. Load carrying housing of rugged design to prevent distortion. Differential and bevel gears supported on taper roller bearings.

Final Drive: From unit power plant, engine torque is transmitted through two plate clutch, four speed transmission, metal universal joints, two piece tubular propeller shaft with self-aligning sealed intermediate bearing to spiral bevel drive, full floating rear axle. Driving and braking stresses are absorbed through ball mounted radius rods fastened to substantial frame brackets at front end and to spring seats on rear axle at rear.

Frame: Carbon steel heat treated frame of extra deep channel section—7 7/8" deep, 4" wide (maximum) and 5/16" thick.

Springs: Semi-elliptic front springs—38" long—2 1/2" wide. Rear springs shackled at front and rear with auxiliary spring contacting with heavy brackets on frame. Rear spring 3" wide—56" long.

Wheels: Budd spoke type wheel.

Brakes: Service—Mechanical self-energizing four wheel brakes with vacuum booster, giving easy pedal action. Front Brakes—16 x 2 1/2 and rear brakes—17 1/4 x 3 internal expanding on cast brake drums—fully enclosed. Parking—14" disc type brake mounted on driveshaft at rear of transmission operated by hand lever at right of gear shift lever.

Front Axle: Drop forged "I" beam section axle—amply designed to take severe braking stresses. Reverse Elliott type with roller thrust bearing at pivot pin. Taper roller bearings at wheels.

Steering Gear: Irreversible type—providing easy steering and exceptional maneuverability in traffic. Steering wheel 18" diameter with non-metallic rim.

Standard Equipment: Speedometer, engine temperature indicator, oil pressure gauge, ammeter, gasoline gauge mounted on instrument board. Spare rim and tire carrier under rear of frame. Electric horn with horn button on steering column. Air filter and oil filter on engine. Full set of electric lights. Heavy duty battery. Rear tow hooks and front bumper. Auxiliary rear springs and dual rear tires. Full set tools and jack. All steel cowl, front fenders and steel running boards and shields.

Optional Equipment: An all steel cab is available at an additional price. Bodies and other special equipment furnished to specifications.

Painting: Chassis, bodies and cabs in lead—will be painted to customer's specifications at extra price.

Pierce-Arrow reserves the right to change any of the specifications listed without obligation to subsequent purchasers, or to add new designs or improvements without making similar alterations in trucks already manufactured.

**Longer wheelbases will be furnished at extra cost and on specific approval of factory.*

A 1932 advertisement for a White Motor–made "Pierce-Arrow" truck. An eight-cylinder engine was used. (Courtesy of the Pierce-Arrow Society.)

The Travelodge, in 1937, was made in three sizes, as Models A, B, and C.
(Courtesy of the Pierce-Arrow Society.)

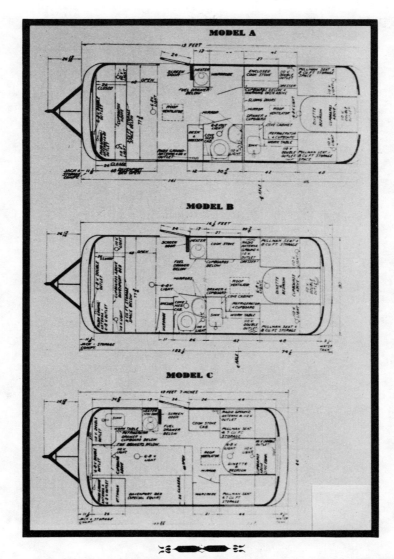

Top—The floor plans of the three models of Travelodge (1937). (Courtesy of the Pierce-Arrow Society.)
Bottom left and right—The steel frame of the Travelodge was covered with sheet aluminum. The junction of these
dissimilar metals caused considerable corrosion to occur. (Courtesy of the Pierce-Arrow Society.)

219

10
THE
PIERCE ARROW SOCIETY

The last Pierce-Arrow was made in 1938. Dealerships ceased and available parts began to dwindle. Pierce-Arrows continued to be driven, but their numbers became fewer. Because of their high-quality, many of the engines were removed to power other machines (stationary types). Some cars became tow trucks or other commercial workhorses. The demand for scrap steel during World War II also took its toll on the large, gas-guzzling cars. Gradually the Pierce-Arrows disappeared from used-car lots and the last of them went to sleep in old garages under blankets of dust.

The collecting of antique cars grew slowly. At first, old-car collectors were regarded as being slightly crazy. The Horseless Carriage Club of America (H.C.C.A.) formed on November 14, 1937, was the first United States organization of antique-car lovers. The Veteran Motor Car Club of America (V.M.C.C.A.) was formed December 2, 1938. The number of collectors remained relatively small until the late 1960s and early 1970s. The profit motive supplanted the "love of old cars and their history."

In 1957 a small group of car enthusiasts led by R. Vale Faro banded together to encourage the preservation and restoration of Pierce-Arrow automobiles, conduct tours, and provide a means for the exchange of information. Faro was the editor of the new Pierce-Arrow Society's publication. This quarterly publication, *The Arrow*, grew to be a quality source of information and enjoyment under the guidance of editors Wally Petersen, Mary Hecht, and Bernard Weis.

The society has adopted a logo consisting of three of the hallmarks of the automobile: the hexagon; the fender headlamp; and the pierced arrows. The organization has an annual meeting for the display of automobiles, awarding of prizes and exchange of technical information. The 1978 meet celebrated the hundredth anniversary of the founding of the George M. Pierce Company and was held in Buffalo, New York, the home of Pierce-Arrow Company.

Of the approximately 85,000 Pierce vehicles produced, it is estimated that fewer than 2,000 survive (figures from Del De Rees). Club members' holdings account for about 900 cars, bicycles and motorcycles. At the 1978 meet, 140 Pierce vehicles were displayed, and included bicycles, Travelodges, motorcycles and a truck. Nearly every production year was represented.

The Pierce-Arrow Society welcomes anyone, owner or not, who has an interest in Pierce-Arrow. Further information can be obtained from:

> Mr. Bernard Weis, Editor
> *The Arrow*
> 135 Edgerton Street
> Rochester, New York 14607

Top—Ladies' Pierce bicycle, circa 1900. (Owner Bob Lyons.) *Bottom*—1912 four-cylinder Pierce motorcycle. (Owner Ed Gibes.)

Top — 1903 Pierce Motorette. (From the Harrah Automobile Collection.) *Bottom* — 1903 Pierce Stanhope.
(Owner Mark Sandoro.) 1905 Great Arrow in background. (Owner Henry Austin Clark.)

Top — 1906 Great Arrow, Model 28-32NN. (Owner Richard Teague.) *Bottom* — Rare original 1908 Great Arrow. (From the Los Angeles County Museum.)

Top — 1907 Great Arrow, Model 45-PP. (Owner John Hovey.) *Bottom* — 1911 Pierce-Arrow, Model 36-UU. (Owner Richard Pettingell.)

Top — 1931 Town Car, Model 41. It was the New York show car. (Owner Gordon Tucker.)
Bottom — 1931 Phaeton, Model 43. (Owner Wally Rank.)

Top—Author's 1917, 38-C-4 Town Brougham. (Formerly of the Zimmerman Collection.)
Bottom—Author's 1932 Model 54 five-passenger Sedan.

227

Appendix A: Pierce-Arrow Chronology

1846 George N. Pierce is born.

1873 Pierce helps establish the firm of Heintz, Pierce, and Munschauer.

1878 The George N. Pierce Company is formed.

1892 Pierce Company begins building bicycles.

1900 Pierce experiments with steam vehicles. Experimental gasoline vehicle built.

1901 Fergusson builds two Motorettes for Pierce. Motorette put into production.

1903 Stanhope model introduced. "Arrow" model introduced, and Won two gold medals in New York–Pittsburgh endurance run.

1904 "Great Arrow" introduced. Designer James Way develops cast-aluminum body for Great Arrow.

1905 First Glidden trophy won.

1906 Elmwood Plant built.

1907 New six-cylinder engine used in Great Arrow. Percy Pierce manages separate Pierce Bicycle Co.

1909 George Pierce retires; George Birge becomes President. Company name changed to "Pierce-Arrow Motor Car Company." Four-cylinder motorcycle introduced.

1910 George Pierce dies.
Air pump introduced on cars.

1911 First truck introduced (5-ton).

1912 Four doors are standard.

1913 Compressed air starter is available. Electric lights and generator become standard.

1914 Fender headlights are optional. Electric starter put on Series 2 cars. Pressurized gasoline feed used. Bicycle and motorcycle business fails.

1916 President Birge retires; Clifton becomes president. Pierce stock goes public. Series 4 cars have thermostat to regulate engine temperature.

1918 Big "66" engine goes out of production. New dual-valve engine introduced in Series 5 cars. President Clifton replaced by John Jay, Jr.

1919 George Goethals Company retained to manage Pierce-Arrow.

1920 George Mixter replaces John Jay as president. All new Series 32 introduced with left-hand steering.

1921 Goethals firm disassociates from Pierce-Arrow. Fergusson retires; Mixter leaves. Slip differential patent issued to Francis Davis.

1922 Myron Forbes becomes president.

1924 Model 80 (light "six") introduced. Four wheel brakes are available.

1926 Experimental aluminum cars built by Pierce-Arrow for Alcoa. Davis invents power steering (on his 1921 Pierce-Arrow).

1928 Colonel Clifton dies. Pierce-Arrow merges with Studebaker. Pierce crest placed on radiator shell of Series 36 and Series 81. Fleet Arrow truck introduced. Helmeted archer appears on radiator.

1929 All new body styles introduced with eight-cylinder "L" type engine. Safety glass used. Forbes resigns and is replaced by Albert Erskine from Studebaker.

1931 Free wheeling introduced; bareheaded archer appears.

1932 All truck production stopped, and White Motor Corporation resumes building "Pierce" trucks. V-12 engine developed; Startix used.

1933 Merger with Studebaker dissolves, and Buffalo businessmen buy Pierce-Arrow for $1,000,000. Erskine commits suicide. Five famous Silver Arrows built. Ab Jenkins breaks speed records. Hydraulic valve lifters first used.

1934 Production of Silver Arrows begun. Pierce-Arrow goes bankrupt.

1935 Loan frees reorganized Pierce-Arrow Motor Corporation from bankruptcy.

1936 Last new model introduced. Travelodge line introduced.

1938 Pierce-Arrow ceases to function, March 28.

1944 Pierce-Arrow legally dissolved.

1957 Pierce-Arrow Society formed.

Appendix B: Pierce-Arrow Data

Year	Model	Cyl- inders	Bore & Stroke	Engine HP	Wheel Base (inches)	Tire Size (inches)	Engine RPM	Weight (lbs)	Price	Approx. No. Made	Peculiar Characteristics and Notable Features
1901–1902	A	1	$2^{15}/_{16}$ x 3	2¾	58	26		600	$ 750	22	Motorette
1902–1903	D-E	1	$3^{5}/_{32}$ x $3^{5}/_{32}$	3½	58	26		725	$ 850	127	Reverse gear Motorette
1903	5H-K	1	3⅜ x $3^{9}/_{16}$	5	70	28 x 3		800	$ 950	39	Center headlight Motorette
	6H-K	1	$3^{9}/_{16}$ x $4^{5}/_{16}$	6	70	28 x 3		1,000	$1,150	149	4-passenger Stanhope
	8L	1	$3^{15}/_{16}$ x $4^{5}/_{16}$	8	70	30 x 3	1,800	1,250	$1,275	51	
	15J	2	$3^{15}/_{16}$ x $4^{5}/_{16}$	15	81	32		1,650	$2,500	49	Conventional body—"Arrow"
1904	8M	1	$3^{15}/_{16}$ x $4^{5}/_{16}$	8	70	30 x 3	1,800	1,250	$1,275	222	Stanhope—tiller replaced with steering wheel
	15J	2	$3^{15}/_{16}$ x 4¾	15	81	32 x 3½		1,900	$2,500	75	Typical Pierce radiator
	24–28N	4	$3^{15}/_{16}$ x 4¾	24–28	93	34 x 4 (4½)		2,600	$4,000	50	"Great Arrow," aluminum body
1905	24–28N	4	$3^{15}/_{16}$ x 4¾	24–28	100	34 x 4 (4½)		2,600	$3,500	75	
	28–32NN	4	4½ x 4¾	28–32	104–109	34 x 4 (4½)	1,600	2,700	$4,000–$5,000	200	
	40P	4	4⅞ x 5	40	104–109	36 x 4½	1,500	3,000	$5,000	25	
1906	28–32NN	4	4¼ x 4¾	28–32	107	34 x 4½	1,600	2,700	$5,000	400	
	40–45PP	4	5 x 5½	40–45	109	36 x 5	1,500	3,100	$6,250	300	
1907–1908	30NN	4	4¼ x 4¾	30	112	34 x 4	1,600	2,700	$4,000–$5,000	400	Magneto, shock absorbers
	45PP	4	5 x 5½	45	124	36 x 5	1,500	3,860	$5,000–$6,250	500	
	65Q	6	5 x 5½	65	135	36 x 5	1,400	4,150	$6,500	165	
Late 1908	40S	6	4¼ x 4¾	40	130	36 x 4 (5)	1,600	3,760	$5,500	350	
1908–1909	24T	4	$3^{15}/_{16}$ x 4¾	24	111½	32 x 4 (4½)	1,750	2,813	$3,100–$4,000	103	All 1909s had new four speed transmission
	36UU	6	$3^{15}/_{16}$ x 4¾	36	119	34 x 4 (4½)	1,700	3,187	$3,700–$4,700	307	
	40PP	4 sep.	5 x 5½	40	124	36 x 5 (4)	1,500	3,844	$4,100–$5,400	101	
	48SS	6	4½ x 4¾	48	130	36 x 5 (4)	1,600	3,833	$4,700–$6,200	358	
	60QQ	6 sep.	5 x 5½	60	135	36 x 5½ (4½)	1,400	4,283	$6,000–$7,200	84	
	30U	6	3¾ x 3¾	30	125	34 x 4				3	3 experimental cars, cylinders cast singly
1910	36UU	6	4 x 4¾	36	119 125	36 x 4½	1,700	3,380	$3,850–$5,000	600	Air pump standard
	48SS	6	4½ x 4¾	48	128 134½	37 x 5	1,600	4,120	$4,850–$6,200	800	
	66QQ	6	5¼ x 5½	66	133½ 140	38 x 5½	1,400	4,500	$5,850–$7,200	100	
1911	36UU	6	4 x 5⅛	36	119 127½	36 x 4½	1,700	3,380	$4,000–$5,500	1,000	Front doors on touring car
	48SS	6	4½ x 5½	48	128 134½	37 x 5	1,600	4,120	$4,850–$6,200	1,000	

Year	Model	Cyl-inders	Bore & Stroke	Engine HP	Wheel Base (inches)	Tire Size (inches)	Engine RPM	Weight (lbs)	Price	Approx. No. Made	Peculiar Characteristics and Notable Features
	66QQ	6	5¼ x 5½	66	133 / 140	38 x 5½	1,400	4,500	$5,850–$7,200	205	
1912	36UU	6	4 x 5⅛	36	119 / 127½	36 x 4½	1,700	3,850	$4,000–$4,900	1,000	Electric generator
	48SS	6	4½ x 5½	48	128 / 134½	37 x 5	1,600	4,675	$4,850–$6,100	833	
	66QQ	6	5 x 7	66	133 / 140	38 x 5½	1,400	5,000	$5,850–$7,100	202	
1913	38C	6	4 x 5½	38	127½ / 132	36 x 4½	1,700	4,200	$4,300–$5,200	750	Compressed air starter, electric headlights, top hood ventilators
	48B	6	4½ x 5½	48	134½ / 142	37 x 5	1,700	4,960–5,450	$4,850–$6,300	825	
	48D	6	4½ x 5½	48	134½	37 x 5	1,600		$5,000	134	7-passenger touring
	66A	6	5 x 7	66	140 / 147½	38 x 5½	1,500	5,440	$5,850–$7,300	199	
1914	C-Series 2	6	4 x 5½	38	127½ / 132	36 x 4½	1,800	4,300	$4,300–$5,400	503	
	B-Series 2	6	4½ x 5½	48	134½ / 142	37 x 5	1,700	5,000	$4,850–$6,300	900	Fender headlights first appeared, Electric starter
	A-Series 2	6	5 x 7	66	140 / 147½	38 x 5½	1,500	5,500	$5,850–$7,300	65 (150)	
1914–1916	C-Series 3	6	4 x 5½	38	134	36 x 4½	2,000	4,400	$4,300–$5,350	1,650	
	B-Series 3	6	4½ x 5½	48	142	37 x 5	1,800	5,100	$4,900–$6,250	1,350	
	A-Series 3	6	5 x 7	66	147	38 x 5½	1,600	5,500	$5,900–$7,200	100	
1916–1918	C-Series 4	6	4 x 5½	38	134	36 x 4½	2,000	4,300	$4,300–$5,200	2,004	Electric clock
	B-Series 4	6	4½ x 5½	48(72)	142	37 x 5½	1,800	5,100	$5,000–$6,000	2,400	
	A-Series 4	6	5 x 7	66(92)	147½	38 x 5½	1,600	5,500	$6,000–$7,000	505	
1918–1919	B-Series 5	6	4½ x 5½	48(143)	142	36⅝ x 5⅜	2,500	5,100	$6,400–$8,200	1,000	Dual valve engine
1919–1920	31	6	4 x 5½	38	134	36 x 4	2,600	4,300	$7,250–$8,750	1,750	
	51	6	4½ x 5½	48	142	36¾ x 5¾	2,500	5,100	$7,650–$9,450	2,250	
1921	32	6	4 x 5½	38.4 (85)	138	36¾ x 5¾	300		$6,500–$8,500	1,000	EnBlock engine, steering wheel on left side
1922–1924	33	6	4 x 5½	38.4 (85)	138	33 x 5	3,000	4,500–5,000	$5,200–$7,000	6,580	
1925	33	6	4 x 5½	38.4 (83)	138	33 x 5	3,000	4,500–5,000	$5,200–$7,000	5,654	"L" type engine
	80	6	3½ x 5	70	130	32 x 5¾	2,800		$2,500–$4,000		
1926–	36	6	4 x 5½	100	138	33 x 6¾	3,000	4,700	$5,800–$8,000	11,860	

Year	Model	Cylinders	Bore & Stroke	Engine HP	Wheel Base (inches)	Tire Size (inches)	Engine RPM	Weight (lbs)	Price	Approx. No. Made	Peculiar Characteristics and Notable Features
1927											
	80	6	3½ x 5	70	130	32 x 5¾	2,800		$2,495–$4,050		
1928											
	36	6	4 x 5½	100	138	33 x 6¾	3,000	4,500–4,700	$5,875–$8,000	5,492	
	81	6	3½ x 5	29.4 (75)	130	32 x 6	3,200	3,100–3,700	$3,100–$3,500		
1929											
	133	8	3½ x 4¾	39.2 (125)	133	31 x 6½	3,200	4,100–4,550	$2,775–$3,500	9,840	New 8 cylinder engine
	143	8	3½ x 4¾	39.2 (125)		32 x 7	3,200	4,500–4,700	$3,750–$8,200		
1930											
	A	8	3½ x 5	132	144	18 x 7.00	3,800	4,500–4,885	$2,775–$3,500		
	B	8	3½ x 4¾	125	134–139	18 x 7.00	3,800	4,300–4,830		6,916	
	C	8	3⅜ x 4¾	115	132	19 x 6.50	3,800	4,450–4,520	$8,200		
1931											
	43	8	3½ x 4¾	125	134–137	19 x 6.50	3,800	4,320–4,820			
	42	8	3½ x 5	132	142	18 x 7.00				4,500	
	41	8	3½ x 5	132	147	18 x 7.00		4,780–5,200			
1932											
	54	8	3½ x 4¾	125	137–142	18 x 7.00	3,800	4,650–5,100	$2,385–$3,050		
	53	12	3¼ x 4	140	137–142	18 x 7.00	3,200		$3,185–$3,850	2,692	New V-12 engine
	52	12	3⅜ x 4	150	142–147	18 x 7.00	3,200	5,400–5,500	$3,785–$4,250		
	51	12	3⅜ x 4	150	147	18 x 7.00	3,200				
1933											
	836	8	3½ x 4¾	135	136–139	17 x 7.00	3,400	4,600–5,000			
	1236	12	3⅜ x 4	160	136–139	17 x 7.00	3,400	4,700–5,100		2,152	Automatic power brakes
	1242	12	3½ x 4	175	137–142	17 x 7.40	3,400	5,100–5,500			
	1247	12	3½ x 4	175	147	17 x 7.50	3,400	5,200–5,800			
	SIL ARR	12	3⅜ x 4	175	139	17 x 7.00	3,400	5,729		5	
1934											
	836A	8	3½ x 4¾	135	136	17 x 7.00	3,400	4,700–4,900			
	840A	8	3½ x 5	140	139–144	17 x 7.00	3,400	4,800–5,200		1,740	Hydraulic valve lifters, custom Brunn bodies
	1240A	12	3½ x 4	175	139–144	17 x 7.50	3,400	5,100–5,500			
	1248A	12	3½ x 4	175	147	17 x 7.50	3,400				
1935											
	845	8	3½ x 5	140	139–144	17 x 7.00	3,400	5,000			
	1245	12	3½ x 4	175	139–144	17 x 7.50	3,400	5,400		875	Hydraulic valve lifters, automatic power brakes
	1255	12	3½ x 4	175	147	17 x 7.50	3,400				

Year	Model	Cyl-inders	Bore & Stroke	Engine HP	Wheel Base (inches)	Tire Size (inches)	Engine RPM	Weight (lbs)	Price	Approx. No. Made	Peculiar Characteristics and Notable Features
1936	1601	8	3½ x 5	150	139	17 x 7.00		5,700			
	1602	12	3½ x 4	185	139–144	17 x 7.50		5,900		787	Overdrive, Bendix vacuum boost brakes, automatic starter and choke
	1603	12	3½ × 4	185	147	17 × 7.50		6,000			
1937	1701	8	3½ x 5	150	139–144–147	17 x 7.00		5,800		167	
	1702	12	3½ x 4	185	139–144	17 x 7.50		5,900			
	1703	12	3½ x 4	185	147	17 x 7.50		6,000			
1938	1801	8	3½ x 5	150	138–144–147	17 x 7.00		5,800		17	
	1802	12	3½ x 4	185	138–144	17 x 7.50		5,900			
	1803	12	3½ x 4	185	147	17 x 7.50		6,000			

Bibliography

Brierley, Brooks T. "Pierce-Arrow in the Thirties." *The Arrow,* Fall 1973, pp. 2–7.

Brierley, Brooks T. "Pierce-Arrow in the Teens and Twenties." *The Arrow,* Fall 1975.

Donovan, Frank R. *Wheels for a Nation.* New York: Crowell, 1965.

Dunn, W. S., Jr., ed. "The Pierce-Arrow Motor Car Company." *Niagara Frontier* 25, no. 3 (1978): 1–84.

Hegge, Robert D. "The 1919 Model." *Car Classics,* October 1976, pp. 27–29.

Hendry, Maurice D. "The Twenties—The Turn of the Tide." *Car Classics,* October 1976, pp. 32–37.

Hendry, Maurice D. *Pierce-Arrow.* New York: Ballantine Books, 1971.

Hodgdon, T. A. "The Pierce Four—The Vibrationless Motor Cycle." *The Arrow,* Winter 1977, pp. 7–18.

Huntington, Roger, "Pierce: What of the Engine?" *Car Classics,* December 1976, pp. 40–43.

Langworth, Richard M. "Pierce-Arrow: Three Decades, One Standard of Excellence." *Car Classics,* October 1976, pp. 20–25.

Schroeder, Joseph J. *The Wonderful World of Automobiles, 1895–1930,* Northfield, Illinois: Digest Books, 1971.

The Pierce-Arrow Motor Car Company. *The Flight of the Arrow.* Buffalo, New York: The Whitney-Graham Company, 1933.

Thomas, William H. B. "President Woodrow Wilson and His Pierce-Arrow." *Augusta Historical Bulletin* 9, no. 1 (Spring 1973): pp. 44–57.

Weis, Bernard J. "Frog-Eyes' Father." *Car Classics,* October 1976, pp. 44–45.

INDEX